The Legend of Dyllbert the Pirate ©

"The Road to Piracy"

Book One in a Series of Historical and Hysterical Cartoon Adventures
featuring Portsmouth's very own 19th Century Pirate:
Captain Ignatious Dyllbert!

This Book is Dedicated to the Loving Memory of: Frank's Beloved Mum & Sister Wendy
Pete's Beloved Mum & his Great Friend & Mentor Styx (Les Harding).

Published by WD Publishing
(a division of WD Enterprises, Portsmouth).

Printed and bound in England by
Acme Printing Co. Ltd,
Middle Street, Portsmouth, Hampshire.

Produced by WD Enterprises & WD Publishing,
St John's, 69A Ebery Grove, Copnor,
Portsmouth, Hampshire PO3 6HG.

First Published 1997.

Copyright © WD Enterprises 1997.

ISBN 0 - 9531112 - 0 - 2

Artworks & Layouts by Pete Wallace.
Story Devised & Written by Frank Dunbar.

Without whom ....

◆ Jenny, Pauline and our families for their unswerving love,
support, sacrifice and encouragement ...

◆ Peter Goodship, Annabelle Boyes and Brian Patterson of
Portsmouth Historic Dockyard for their belief, and a big
thank you to Brian for allowing us to use his excellent
artworks ...

◆ Paul Spooner and Peter Hammond of Portsmouth City
Council for their unwavering conviction ...

◆ Keith (Mr. Riddles) Ridley, a true champion and friend ...

◆ The News for giving us the first opportunity ...

◆ Katy Ball and the staff of The City Museum for all their
time devoted to research on our behalf ...

◆ Derek Beaves of George Gale & Co Ltd ...

◆ David Nicholas for his advice & friendship ...

◆ Ron Burch, Erika, and Michelle of SITA Engineering
Efficiency Ltd for their help in producing the draft copy ...

◆ The Midland Bank, Cosham for listening ...

◆ Everyone at HTS Focused Solutions Ltd ...

◆ Rebus Advertising & Design ...

... our heartfelt thanks.

Foreword
by Brian Patterson - Curator and Keeper of Artifacts
for Portsmouth Royal Dockyard Historical Trust.

Portsmouth is a City of great historical interest particularly since, for most of its life, it was a military garrison surrounded by fortifications who's gates were securely locked each and every night.

Today, 54 batteries, forts and castles litter the Solent area, erected for the defence of the Dockyard, testifying to its importance to the British nation as a whole.

The British Empire was founded on the bow-waves of ships of the Royal Navy who's anchorage at Spithead were viewed from Portsmouth Point beach and from the Town fortifications.

Portsmouth Dockyard itself is the oldest of the British navy's establishments with a history that can be traced back to the thirteenth century and which, for nearly two hundred years, was one of the largest industrial complexes in the world. Sadly, little is known of its superb industrial achievements or of its civilian workforce and their families who over the centuries have helped to shape Portsmouth into the wonderful City it is today. A City where even the road and street names have a story to tell. The difficulty is in the telling of such story's for they are so vast and, at times, complex.

Pete Wallace and Frank Dunbar go some way in achieving this in their new book, "The Road to Piracy" which follows the legendary cartoon adventures of Captain Ignatious Dyllbert and his motley crew and is tremendous fun. The historical characters, so cleverly woven into the storylines are not only entertaining but, with events packed with historical facts, are also essentially educational.

I have had the privilege of seeing the Wallace and Dunbar partnership at work and can therefore admire their attention to detail in weaving historical facts into their cartoon strips. (Yes, there really was a Portsmouth to London Stagecoach called the "Rocket".)

Many of the Dockyard and Town scenes are drawn from plans and pictures of the period and I can verify the painstaking research undertaken to get it right. I am convinced that, after reading "The Road to Piracy" you will look forward (as I do) to enjoying further legendary adventures of Dyllbert the Pirate.

Few Cities can boast home bred cartoon characters and I am sure Portsmouth can, and will, be proud of Dyllbert and his motley crew especially as they so wonderfully help to portray the 19th Century History of the Royal Navy, the City of Portsmouth and its Dockyard.

Part one

A short (ish) History and Genealogy of the Portsmouth Region

or

"Did you know that, not a lot of people know that ..."

... *in the beginning* for centuries upon centuries and possibly upon even more centuries than that, the Island of Portsmouth (yes, it really is an Island, separated from the mainland by a stretch of water called *Portscreek*) was nothing more than a rather small, yukky and inhospitable piece of swampland property which was of no particular interest to anybody ... (Except perhaps for single celled swamp beings who enjoyed living in yukky swamps!)

Down through the ages however, Portsmouth slowly evolved from its early yukky swampy days into one of the major south coast cities of modern England and an eminently beautiful holiday resort.

Undoubtedly Britain's premier naval port and the home of the most Historic Naval Dockyard in the World, *Portsmouth* is also the name of a proud region that extends to the River Hamble in the West,

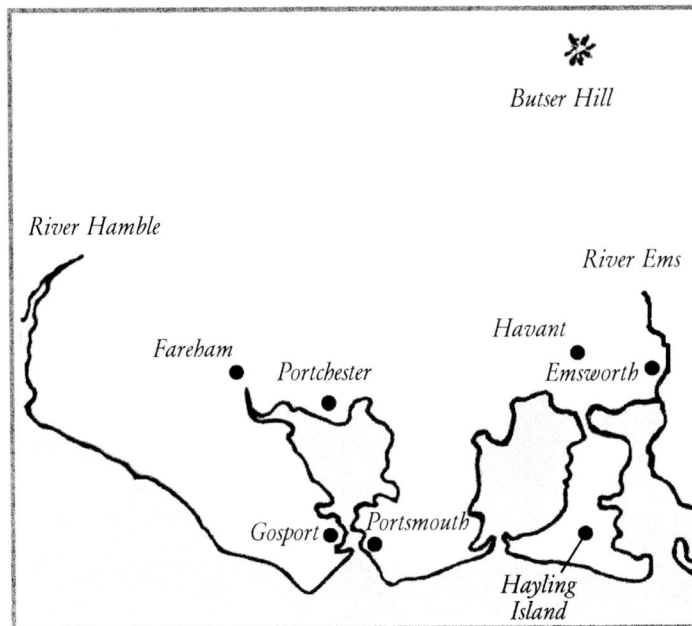

the River Ems in the East, and to the slopes of Butser Hill in the North and also includes the harbour communities of Gosport and Emsworth, as well as the ancient Towns of Havant, Hayling Island and Fareham.

But what of the history of the Portsmouth Region?

When did all the *in the beginning* stuff begin?

And, what were the ages of the aforementioned *down through the ages* bit?

Well, once upon a very long time ago, sometime after ...

The Year Dot BC ...

... when evolution had done its bit, the first regional settlers arrived. They were of course, *the Dinosaurs* who, after several hundred million years of failing to see the potential of developing the area into some sort of *Jurassic Theme Park*, became extinct.

And then somewhere between ...

... droves of Homo Erectus (brutish human type creatures armed with crude flint chopping and cutting tools) began to migrate from Europe, following the herds of game upon which, as hunter gatherers, they were so dependent, and exploiting the region for all it was worth (which, at that time, probably wasn't much more than about 5p).

Naturally, in those far off days, the area (still pretty inhospitable) would not have been known as *The Portsmouth Region* so it's quite likely that, to the vocally challenged Mr & Mrs E, the region would doubtless have been known as: *'Ugg'.*

And then, (taking a quantum leap forward) in about ...

40,000 BC ...

... the first Homo Sapiens-Sapiens (the upwardly mobile forerunner and model for the modern human, and er ... huwoman) appeared in Europe and, like Homo Erectus, also migrated to the region where they finally settled and continued to evolve.

Minding their own business, these European migrants created settlements and quietly got on with taming animals, growing corn, bartering, fighting among themselves, burying their dear departed Chiefs in *Barrows* (no, not wheelbarrows! Earth Barrows, which are early graves), constructing wooden carts, and building humungous stone things that seemed to serve no purpose whatsoever (like for example: *Stonehenge*) ...

... and then approximately 39,000 years later (give or take a millennium or two), in about ...

1000BC ...

... the non-migratory Europeans obviously became bored and so decided to start their *let's invade and conquer another country period.*

And so it was that a bunch of tall, fair haired *Celts* called *Bretons* sailed across the channel from France and, after a quick invading and conquering session, decided to settle, then fell in love with, and ended up conjugating with the native regional tribes-persons, who's offspring naturally became: *Celtic-Bretons.*

A thousand or so years further on, just as the region was settling down and getting used to the idea of being Celtic-Bretons, just as everyone believed all that European invading and conquering stuff was over, who should come along and spoil it all but the *Romans.*

Who, in ...

43AD ...

... by order of *Emperor Claudius,* and without even so much as an *excuse me* or a *by your leave,* invaded and conquered our green and pleasant lands and named our Country; *Brittania* (an apparent spin-off of Breton) which meant of course that all Celtic-Bretons were now classed as: *Celtic-Britons/British.*

In the Portsmouth region, the Romans established a military post at a place they named *Portus Advrni (Portchester)* and, although there is no direct reference to it, were very likely the very first to give the little yukky swampy island settlement that neighboured it, the name of *Portesmutha.* (In fact it is generally believed that Portchester is actually *the Mother of Portsmouth.)*

Over the next 300 years or so of occupation, the Romans founded regional settlements, set up coastal defences, constructed really fabby villas, laid miles of straight roads, introduced bathing and sanitation, built whopping great long walls and also fell in love and conjugated with the local Celtic-Brits, who's offspring then became known as: *Romano-British.*

Then, would you believe it, after three centuries of Roman rule, just as everyone was settling down and getting used to being Romano-Brits, after enjoying the Romans fearless rock solid protection from invasion and attack by any other would be south coast pilfering pirates, such as the Danes and the Saxons etc., what does the Roman Empire do?

It starts to crumble that's what it does, which led to one Roman Legion after another upping kilts, and heading for Rome sweet Rome. (No doubt singing: *'Be it ever so crumbling, there's no place like Rome.')*

... and so it was that by ...

409AD ...

... the whole Roman kit and caboodle had gone leaving the poor old regional Romano-Brits to fend for themselves, which they did quite well, staving off seaborne attacks by the *Angles, Jutes, Danes,* and *Saxons.* Oh yes, they really did quite well.

That is, up until ...

495AD ...

... when the real Saxon conquest began with an invasion led by two warrior chiefs; *Cerdic* and his son *Cynric,* who landed from a small fleet of ships somewhere on the New Forest side of Southampton.

This was followed by the Saxon invasion of Portsmouth which began in ...

501AD ...

... when, according to the *Anglo-Saxon Chronicles,* (and this is obviously not an exact word for word account) ...

'a body of dirty great hairy, and frighteningly bloodthirsty Saxons landed at a place which is called 'Portesmutha' from two large galleys under the command of Port and his two sons, Bieda and Maegla.'

This, apparently, is the earliest recorded historical reference to the actual Island of Portsmouth.

Bravely, the *Portesmuthian* Romano-Brits (concluding these rather boisterous, happy-go-lucky Saxons weren't simply a party of fun-seeking holidaymakers), drew themselves up and opposed them. Unhappily to no use.

The Saxons attacked and, using their favoured weapon, *the shortsword* (which was quite obviously not short enough!), defeated the local Romano-Brits, killed their commander, took possession of the adjoining country and founded settlements all over the Portsmouth region.

And, for the next 600 years of Anglo Saxon rule, (as you have probably guessed by now) they fell in love and conjugated with the Romano-Brits who's offspring presumably became: *Anglo-Saxon-Romano- Brits.*

Then, just as everyone was settling down and happily getting used to being Anglo-Saxon-Romano-Brits, after enjoying their fearless rock solid protection from invasion and attack by any other would be south coast pilfering pirate ...

... (half a mo' isn't this beginning to sound just a tad too familiar) ... along come the perishin' *Normans* who in ...

1066AD ... (900 years incidentally, before England won the world cup at Wembley!!!)

.... led by William *(Billy the Conk)* the Conqueror, invaded, defeated and killed our beloved Saxon ruler, good King Harold, by giving him one (an arrow that is), in the eye.

Thus ended Anglo-Saxon rule and a pretty lengthy Norman rule began.

And, naturally, just like all the others, they also did the falling in love and conjugating bit which made the regional Anglo-Saxon-Romano-Brits, er ... well pretty confused probably!

Anyway, 20 years into his reign, in ...

1086 ...

... King William, being a pretty frugal sort of bloke, ordered the compilation of the *Domesday Book* in order to provide a proper basis for taxation which, much like the old Poll Tax (well any tax really) proved pretty unpopular. Basically, it

listed all the taxable properties of England. All that is *except Portsmouth* which was so insignificant it didn't even rate a mention!

Not that it mattered because, ultimately, the Normans, and in particular *Billy the Conk's* Royal Descendants *King Richard* and *King John,* (without whom a certain *Mr. Robin Hood and his merry men* would never have got their, *rob the rich and give to the poor scheme* off the ground) did actually do the then tiny, but growing island settlement of Portsmouth and its future Dockyard a lot of good.

But not at first.

In fact, development-wise, the area was practically ignored until the 12th c. when it was acquired by the actual founder of Portsmouth, a wealthy Norman merchant by the name of *Jean de Gisors.*

The Development of Portsmouth Town and its Dockyard.

In 1100 and um ... something or other AD ...

... the southernmost part of Portsmouth was still quite marshy and pretty inhospitable.

Even so, the area really attracted Jean de Gisors. Not least because it had a sheltered inlet; a deep water channel protected by a shingle spit that provided a natural harbour and safe haven for his ships and which still exists today and is known as *the Camber area.*

The Camber can be found at the end of Broad Street in Old Portsmouth.

So, anyway in...

1182AD ...

... Henry Plantagenet II, King of all England (oh, and of the French territories of: Normandy, Anjou, Poitou, Guienne, and Gascony) sailed from Portsmouth to France to pacify his son Prince Richard who, along with his friend and ally Philip II Augustus (King of the rest of France) was currently rebelling against him.

Before sailing however, Henry made his will at Portsmouth (which was just as well really because he died in France in 1189 and so never returned to England).

In the meantime in ...

1187AD ...

... Jean de Gisors had laid out the beginnings of *Portsmouth Town,* developing streets and houses around the Camber area and also founding and financing the *Church of St. Thomas,* dedicated to the martyred St. Thomas a'Becket who was murdered by four knights of King Henry II in 1170.

It is now Portsmouth's Cathedral of St. Thomas, and is the finest medieval building in the City.

And then in...

1189AD ...

... following the death of his father, Henry II in France, Richard returned to England, landing at Portsmouth on the 12th August as King of England (and of course: Normandy, Anjou, Poitou etc.) and, shortly after, in ...

1190AD...

... set off with Philip Augustus II on the third leg of the Crusades. (The first leg resulting in a win but the second leg being a bit of a wash out apparently.)

And who knows if a heavyhearted Jean de Gisors himself might not have watched his Monarch's embarkation, waving a hand in tearful and loyal farewell.

He might have ... but um ... he probably didn't!

You see, Prince John, the crusading King's rotten, scheming and cowardly brother saw Richard's absence as a definite career opportunity, and so rebelled against Richard and attempted to claim the throne of England for himself!

And guess who Jean de Gisors chose to support? ...

... *Uh-huh!*

This proved to be a whopping great big boo-boo on the part of Jean de Gisors because, when Prince John failed in his attempted coup, it resulted in poor old Jean being forced to forfeit his lands, including his beloved *Town of Portsmouth*, to King Richard in 1194.

Bad news for dear Jean ... But good news for Portsmouth! For in that same year of ...

1194AD...

... good King Richard again visited Portsmouth but this time on his way to sort out his one time friend and ally,

Philip II Augustus who had nicked most of Richard's French property.

It was then that he granted his *new Portsmouth Town* its first Charter; an historical event recorded in the *Curtis Regis Rolls* which states:

'It pleased the Lord King Richard to build this Town of Portsmouth.'

Naturally that didn't mean he rolled up his sleeves and got stuck in himself with the old bricks and mortar, but he did order the building development of the Town. And he further ordered the construction of a military installation and ... (a quick roll on the drums) ... *a dock!*

The question is; why would Richard *Coeur de Lion* (who, by the way, wore three lions on his shirt long before our beloved English Football Team did), who regarded England as merely a useful inheritance on which to raise money for his crusades, who managed to visit England only twice during his ten year

reign and who could *only speak French,* bother to build a dock in Portsmouth?

Well, firstly he appreciated the immense strategic value of Portsmouth's deep natural harbour and secondly, building such a dock gave him a perfect base for his ships which in turn allowed him to pop across the channel whenever he fancied, to check out his property or mount attacks on France!

Sadly, the legendary King Richard never had the chance to make proper use of his Portsmouth Dock because he was killed in France by a stray arrow in April 1199, which meant of course that bad Prince John became King of England ... ... *(major bummer!)*

However, although John was a nasty, swindling, conniving, devious, (and those were his good points) pretty unloved Monarch, he was not stupid and, like King Richard, could see the potential of having a Dockyard in Portsmouth.

In fact, King John was one of the most frequent of all Royal Visitors to Portsmouth and in ...

1205AD ...

... gathered an amazing fleet of 500 ships in Portsmouth Harbour for an expedition to France in order to prevent Philip II Augustus (yes, him again) from conquering Normandy and all the other parts of his Kingdom in France.

Unfortunately, the expedition had to be abandoned because several nobles who were supposed to take part had a fit of the *sucky-thumb tantrums* and refused to go, resulting in John losing all his French property!

Nevertheless, by this time, Portsmouth had grown from an *in the beginning* insignificant yukky swampy island into a great shipbuilding centre and, due to its magnificent harbour, was the *principal naval base of the Kingdom.*

In fact, by ...

1212AD ...

... it is a pretty safe bet to say that Portsmouth had its first proper Dockyard.

Proof of this comes in the form of a written Royal Command from King John to the Sherriff of Southampton stating:

'We order you, without delay, by the view of lawful men, to cause our Docks at Portsmouth to be enclosed with a Good and Strong Wall in such manner as our beloved and faithful William, Archdeacon of Taunton will tell you, for the preservation of our Ships and Galleys; and likewise to cause penthouses to be made to the same Walls, as the same Archdeacon will also tell you, in which all our Ships tackle may be safely kept; and use as much dispatch as you can, in order that the same may be completed this summer lest in the ensuing winter our Ships and Galleys and their Rigging should incur damage by your default; and when we know the cost it shall be accounted to you.'

This of course is an early form of Cash on Delivery.

Although John had a reputation for being a bad King, he did have a genuine and abiding interest in naval affairs and was undoubtedly a major player in the historic shaping of Portsmouth Town and its Dockyard.

And, albeit his particular docks were short-lived (in May 1228, the docks were flooded by the sea and ordered to be filled in), it has to be said that the first humble beginnings of the *Royal Portsmouth Dockyard* had certainly begun, thanks largely to King John who in ...

1216AD ...

... died.

He was succeeded by his son, Henry the Third, who was only nine at the time and who reigned for an amazing fifty-six years (for some of that time, setting sail from Portsmouth to France, determined to regain the lands lost by his Father King John which, he eventually succeeded in doing). Anyway, Henry died in ...

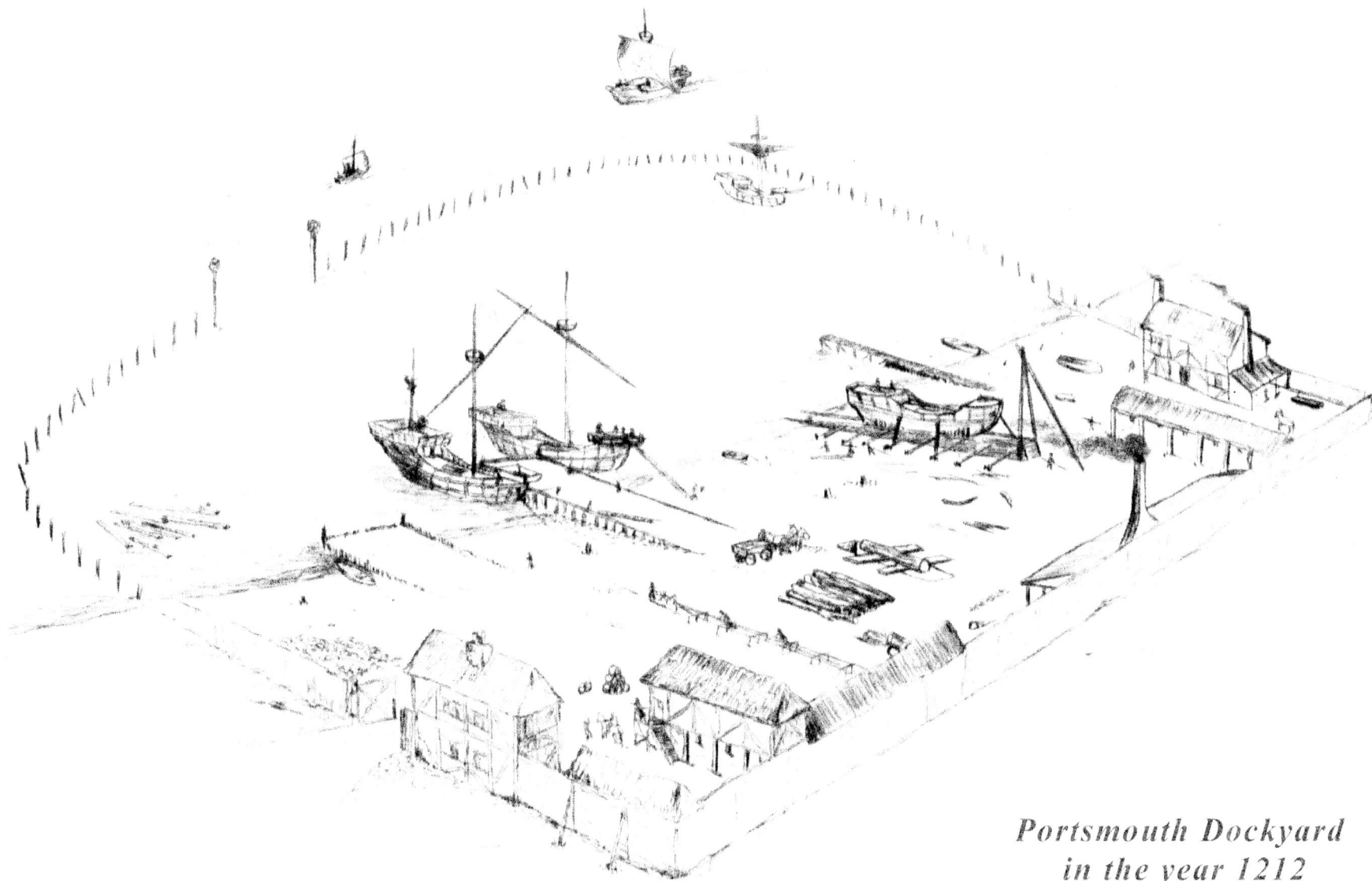

Portsmouth Dockyard in the year 1212

(courtesy: Brian Patterson)

1272AD ...

... and so began the 105 years reign of Edwards I, II, and III. Those years were ticklish times for Portsmouth as the Town was often raided from the sea by *Cinque Port Pirates* and also by the French who in 1337, 1369, and 1372, attacked, looted and then burned the Town to the ground.

However, in ...

1385AD ...

... the rather miffed citizens of Portsmouth Town had their revenge when, at their own expense, they fitted out a small squadron of ships, then set out and engaged and defeated several French squadrons before continuing on across the channel to the Seine and giving the shocked French a right royal, and well deserved, thrashing in their own back yard!

Although at that time, Portsmouth was a favourite port for seaborne attack and for British naval embarkation, very little it seemed was actually being done to improve and develop the Dockyard.

That is, until ...

1431AD ...

... when King Henry V ordered that land be bought for the enlargement of the (*Portsmouth*) Dockyard, to be called: *The Kings Dock.*

Even so, it wasn't until ...

1495AD ...

... that the Dockyard really came into its own. This was the time of King Henry VII, a monarch who so seriously appreciated Portsmouth's obvious advantages as a naval and shipbuilding base, he instructed one *Robert Brygandine* (Clerk of the Ships) to make a dry dock at Portsmouth (sealing once and for all, Portsmouth's destiny as being a major Naval Dockyard and Port).

And so it was, on the 14th June 1495, that work began on the *first ever dry dock in the world.*

The bulk of it was made of wood and it took 46 weeks to build at a princely cost of: £193. 0s. 6¾d.

And on the 25th May in ...

1496AD ...

... the 600 ton *Sovereign* was the first ship to use Portsmouth's dry dock.

She was followed by *The Regent, The Sweepstake* and *The Mary Fortune.*

And then, in ...

1509AD ...

... Henry VII died and was succeeded by the legendary, multi-married, Tudor monarch himself, Henry *(off with her head)* the Eighth.

That same year saw the building, in Portsmouth Dockyard, of the warship *Peter Pomegranate,* which was followed by the construction of one of the most celebrated ships in the world; the Flagship of Henry's Navy; the mighty *Mary Rose!*

And two years later in ...

1511AD ...

... Portsmouth was officially designated as the major building centre for the King's ships.

As for the *Mary Rose,* (Henry's prized ship) well, she served for over 30 meritorious years before that fateful day in ...

1545AD ...

... when she, along with almost the entire English fleet (which was anchored in the Solent), set sail and prepared to face a French (yes, them pesky varmints again) invasion of 200 ships.

Watched in utter horror by King Henry himself from the ramparts of Southsea Castle, the Mary Rose suddenly slewed over, capsized and sank taking 400 crew with her.

By the King's order, many attempts were made to salvage her, but all to no avail. (In fact, she didn't again see the light of day until over 400 years later when, in October 1982, her hull was raised and the Mary Rose was at last returned home to Portsmouth Dockyard, the place of her birth.)

By the time of the tragic sinking of the Mary Rose, Portsmouth was already a heavily fortified garrison town & naval port and, *Britain's premier shield against invasion from France.* Her Dockyard too had also become something of a pretty industrious shipbuilding complex.

That is until about ...

1547AD ...

... during the reign of Edward VI, when things went a wee bit stagnant.

In fact, to put it bluntly, for the next century, Portsmouth and her Dockyard went downhill faster than a greyhound on a skateboard!

And there was much wailing and gnashing of teeth, what with *The Plague of 1563* and the *English Civil War of 1642* and all!

However, by ...

1665AD ...

... major redevelopment was afoot.

On the throne was Charles II (who on May 21st 1662, married his Queen: *Catherine of Braganza* in Portsmouth in the church known as *The Domus Dei,* (which was founded circa 1212 and is now *The Royal Garrison Church*)), and a famous Dutch engineer: *Sir Bernard de Gomme,* was charged with the job of re-planning the fortifications of the Town & Dockyard.

Portsmouth was on its way up at last!

And by ...

1670AD ...

... King Charles had created the *first proper, bona-fide Royal Navy* and had further initiated the major expansion of Portsmouth Dockyard which continued on into the reign of William III.

And so by ...

1698AD ...

... the Great Ship Basin and the Great Stone Dock (No. 5 Dock) had been built, followed two years later by No 6 Dock.

Oh yes, on the development side, things were definitely on the up! And so, incidentally, was the intake of dockyard workers, sailors and, naturally, their families.

So much so in fact that by the reign of Queen Anne in ...

1703AD ...

... a new Town had begun to spring up outside the ramparts of Portsmouth Dockyard to house the growing workforce and their kin.

This new Town was known as *Portsea* and within 100 years, its population had surpassed that of the old walled Town of Portsmouth! (Why do rabbits come to mind?)

In fact, everything was expanding. Including the Dockyard which by ...

1733AD ...

... had increased its size by ten and a half acres, had a new dockyard wall erected, and was, in itself, a *Town within a Town* with its own church, stables, smithery and houses.

There was also an established Naval Academy for the education of *'forty young gentlemen, sons of nobelmen and gentlemen'* who were taught French, Drawing, Fencing, and the use of the Firelock.

It's a shame the Academy didn't also teach these young snobby, wealthy and spoilt young gentlemen, who very soon gained a reputation for idleness, swearing, and drunkenness, how to act like, well .... gentlemen!

Anyway, in ...

1797AD ...

... war (with ... guess who? .... yes, that's right ... France) was at its height. *Mad King George III* was on the throne, *Admiral Lord Nelson* was a major hero and *Midshipman Ignatious Dyllbert* (the future Dyllbert the Pirate) was serving under *Admiral Gardner* aboard the *Royal Sovereign* and involved in the *Spithead Mutiny*.

And Portsmouth? Well, Portsmouth was now Britain's foremost naval station and her Dockyard had become the world's largest, self contained industrial complex.

Not bad for a one time, insignificant yukky swampy little island, eh?

Particularly as in ...

The Royal Dockyard at Portsmouth

1787

(courtesy of Brian Patterson)

Slip way

Slip way

Bricklayers Yard

Shed

The New Buildings

Garden

Fish / horse Pond

Stables

Work Shed

Timber Berths

Boat Troughs

Slip way

Boat Pond

Porter Row Officers Quarters

Dockyard wall

Portsea Town

Garden

Seasoning Shed

Reasoning Shed

Boat House

Slip way

Boat House

Long Row Officers Quarters

Weigh House

Lighting House

St Annes Church

The Commissioners House

The Academy

Crane

Bridge

Store

Timber Berths

Statue of King William

French House

Garden

Crane

Bridge

North Chamber

Prussian deal Store

Store

Timber Berths

Mould Loft

Hanging House

The Green

Pay Office

Crane

Saw pits

Bridge

The Old North Bason

Store

Saw pitt

Rigging Store

Deal Yard

The Great Rope House

Slip way

Slipway

Slipway

pump

Stone dock

North dock

New dock

Work Shops

Mould Loft

Mast House

Slipway

Mast Pond

pump

The Great Bason

Timber store

Porters lodge gateway

pump

Double dock

Sail loft

Offices

Sea Serving Store

Store

Shop for Tar and pitch

Bridge dock

Mast houses

Pitch House Jetty

Tar House

Rope House

Camber

South dock

Sail loft

Deal Yard

North Store

Middle Store

South Store

Bridge

Kings Store

Work Sheds

Island

Mast Pond

Camber

Sail loft

Rigging House

Anchor Pond

Sail field

The Watering Island

17

The Legend of Dyllbert the Pirate

"Tis 1804. Britain is at war with France and Inventor Silas Smutt works on his secret invention in The Great Ship Basin at ..."

PORTSMOUTH DOCKYARD

Pass me a two inch spanner Mr Plank.

'Ere ain't it time you were off ter **London** Mr Smutt?

Lawks! I forgot about that! **Quick** hail me a Sedan!

Righto Mr Smutt!

Mr Smutt! You've forgotten summink.

The Blue Posts m'lads, and step on it!

THE BLUE POSTS - Broad Street

Stop 'im Alf (gasp), he's forgotten ter pay!!

Hold that coach!!

Well Ma'am, I was so involved with my work, I near forgot my meeting at The Admiralty!!

You are a most forgetful man Mr Smutt ...

... Pray look into my hand-mirror and note that you have also forgotten ...

Aaarrrgghh!!

... to WASH!!

Perhaps m'Lords won't notice!!!

Dyllbert the Pirate's Fact File

The Great Ship Basin

Also known as No 1 Basin, the Great Ship Basin in Portsmouth Dockyard did, and still does exist and can be found adjacent to Admiral Lord Horatio Nelson's world famous Flagship, HMS Victory.

Built in 1698 (the year Peter the Great of Russia visited Portsmouth Dockyard), and enlarged during the years 1795-1801, the Great Ship Basin was an integral part of the ship building process.

New ships were first constructed in a slipway after which they would be floated into one of the Great Ship Basin's six dry docks for fitting out.

Once that was completed, the ship would then be floated into the Basin itself to be put through initial trials before being taken out of Portsmouth Harbour and into the Solent for rigorous sea trials.

The Blue Posts

The Blue Posts Hotel, where Silas Smutt caught his coach to London, was an actual coaching house situated in Broad Street, Portsmouth.

Built in 1613 it was distinguished by its large, bright blue posterns which flanked the entrances to the bar and stable yard.

Also a popular watering hole for Midshipmen and naval personnel of lesser rank it was destroyed by fire in 1870.

The Legend of Dyllbert the Pirate

"Inventor Silas Smutt visits the Flag Officer Prototype Ships and Admiral Lord Nelson with some very exciting news! ..."

LONDON 1804 - Admiralty House

LORD BYRON PUDD

F.O.P.S.

Well Mr Smutt ... is she ready?

That she is Lord Pudd, berthed at **Portsmouth** awaiting her sea-trials ...

...With my **steam powered** paddle vessel, Lord Nelson will have the most powerful ship in the world!!

My congratulations Mr Smutt. She will be a far better flagship for me than the **Victory** ...

... and I shall be pleased to test her thoroughly myself.

EEEK!!

Methinks you should choose someone **expendable** to do that!!!

How so Mr Smutt?

Well Lord Nelson ... **SHE JUST MIGHT BLOW UP!**

Oddsbods!

Dyllbert the Pirate's Fact File

H.M.S. Victory

Admiral Lord Horatio Nelson's illustrious Flagship (1803-1805) H.M.S. Victory is undoubtedly the most celebrated historic warship in the world.

Costing £63,176. 15s and launched in 1765, she is 226ft. 6in (69 metres) long, 51ft. 10in (16 metres) wide, and weighs 2,162 tons.

Classified a 'Ship o' the Line' (Battleship), she had a ships compliment of 850 officers and men (150 of which were Marines), and a pretty devastating firepower of 104 guns.

A little known fact is that not all Victory's sailors were British. Indeed, at Trafalgar, at least 20 other Countries were represented including: Africa, America and Russia!

In 1812 she was 'paid off' at Portsmouth and between 1813 - 16, was rebuilt. She became the Flagship of the Commander in Chief, Portsmouth in 1889, and remains so to this day.

In 1922, after 157 years of truly meritorious service, this grand old lady was berthed in No 2 Dock in Portsmouth Dockyard where (still a fully commissioned warship) she continues to reside, serving as a fitting and unique tribute to, not only Admiral Lord Nelson, but to the remarkably heroic ordinary seamen of a bygone age.

The Legend of Dyllbert the Pirate

"Lords Pudd and Nelson are shocked to learn that Silas Smutt's untested steamship might blow up ..."

ADMIRALTY HOUSE - London

Rest assured gentlemen, I shall choose an **utterly expendable** Captain for the steamship trials!

Most wise Lord Pudd. And now I must return to Portsmouth.

Of course Mr Smutt. **LIEUTENANT PROD!**

Ah, Prod. Kindly escort Mr Smutt from the building.

Phew! They didn't notice my **unwashed appearance!**

We shall meet again in **Portsmouth Dockyard** on the day of the sea-trials.

Very well Lord Pudd.

... and **please wash** before that day Mr Smutt.

Blast!!

If Smutt's steamship does blow up, t'will be a sad loss to the Admiralty!

And a sad loss of the brave Captain commanding her, Byron!

Not necessarily!!

Character Profile

Silas Smutt

The designer and inventor of the remarkable steam powered wonder ship destined to be Admiral Lord Nelson's new Flagship, was born on the Isle of Wight in 1760.

An habitual tinkerer, Smutt is permanently covered in grime from head to chest!

At the tender and impressionable age of 12, he was apprenticed to, and studied engineering design, theory and practise under the tuition, and watchful eye of the legendary Scottish engineer and inventor, James Watt.

Sadly, although very good at theory, in practise Smutt leaves a lot to be desired.

In fact, many of his personal steam engine designs have ended in utter disaster, ie they exploded! (Thankfully without injury or loss of life.) Consequently, Smutt has a tendancy to use (steal) engine designs that are not necessarily his own!

Nonetheless, Smutt does eventually become an excellent and talented engineer in his own right, solving many a tricky problem as well as designing a whole gamut of amazing steam powered devices.

The Legend of Dyllbert the Pirate

"Lord Pudd chooses an expendable Captain to command the sea trials of Inventor Silas Smutt's potentially dangerous prototype steamship ..."

I know the very man for the task, Horatio!

Really Byron! To whom do you refer?

a Captain **so useless in the art of navigation** he is incapable of all but patrolling Solent water ...

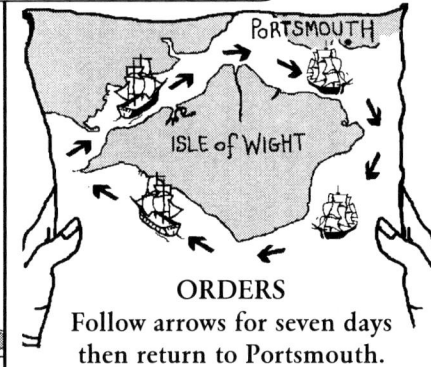

PORTSMOUTH

ISLE of WIGHT

ORDERS
Follow arrows for seven days then return to Portsmouth.

... who would be lost were he to lose sight of Southern England ...

OH NO! Where's the South Coast gone?

It's over 'ere Cap'n.

... a Captain who is sea-sick more than you, Horatio...

More than me! Then say no more Byron!!

... for only one fits that description ...

Land Ho lads, and **guess where!**

It wouldn't 'appen to be **Portsmouth** again, would it?

... **Captain Ignatious Dyllbert!!**

Oh Lord! (burp) Please make the Admiralty give me a shore post (barff).

Dyllbert the Pirate's Fact File

Nelson - The Ultimate Seaman?

Few would deny that Nelson was a born seaman. So much so in fact, the lifeblood that flowed through his veins, the very lifeblood he valiantly spilled for love of Country must have been at least 90% sea-water.

He was a true Lord of the Sea, a 19th century Naval superstar (who, incidentally, was so beloved and idolized by the entire British nation he could quite easily have outdone 'Elvis', 'The Beatles', or 'Oasis', in the popularity stakes).

Although slight of build and physically and visually challenged he was a literal super-seaman, respected and revered by all who served under him, and who even today, is an inspiration to sailors the world over. It is strange to relate therefore that this Lord of the Sea, this British Naval Legend (who even Neptune and Poseidon, the ancient Roman and Greek Gods of the sea would have admired), actually suffered from ... seasickness!

Yes, Nelson may have been 'the ultimate seaman' and the greatest Naval Commander of his time, but he was also a pretty poor sailor!

So, the next time you're aboard a Ship or a Ferryboat and you begin to feel horribly queasy, just you remember Lord Nelson. Because, if being a seasick sailor was good enough for that Heroic Naval Legend, then it must surely be good enough for you too!

The Legend of Dyllbert the Pirate

"A very seasick Captain Dyllbert, unaware of Lord Pudd's plans for him, has put his ship, *H.M.S. Nauseas*, in for supplies at ..."

THE VICTUALLING YARD - Gosport

Cap'n Dyllbert! T'is I, Bosun Squint ...

Oh no!! Not the Navy's smelliest sailor!!!

ENTER SQUINT, but keep your whiffy body well away from my conk!

A signal from the Admiralty Cap'n.

Oh joy! A reply to my shore-posting request! **Throw it to me Squint!!**

Pooh, what a smelly signal. You didn't perchance drop it into a box of rotting fish?

No Cap'n. 'Twere stuffed inside me shirt, under me armpit!!!

Under your armpit Squint! Ye Gods!! I dread to think what foul contagious things might lurk there!

Oh Lor'! and I touched the signal!!

If my fingers **drop off** Squint, you'll swing from the yard-arm by your **scrawny little neck!**

Oooer!!!

Character Profile

Captain Ignatious Dyllbert RN

Ignatious Josiah Dyllbert was born in Portsmouth circa 1780, and is the loving son of the late lamented Admiral Josiah Ignatious Dyllbert RN and Mrs. Millicent Dyllbert.

With his fathers help and support, Dyllbert entered the service as a twelve year old Midshipman and shortly after wished that he hadn't for, as Dyllbert soon discovered, whenever the sea heaved, his stomach would invariably heave right along with it.

Although, over the years Dyllbert learned to love the Navy, his seasickness made him dread going to sea.

So much so in fact, he has, since his early Midshipman days, continuously sent 'shore post' requests to the Admiralty (which, for reasons known only to themselves, the Admiralty chose to ignore!).

A useless navigator, unable to grasp even the basics of this essential craft, Dyllbert nevertheless rose to his present rank of Captain (thanks mainly, it has to be said, by the 'string pulling' of his father).

Naturally, the Admiralty, knowing Dyllbert's navigational limitations, had no intention of trusting him with the command of an ocean going warship ...

The Legend of Dyllbert the Pirate

"Dyllbert fears his fingers will drop off after touching a signal carried under the arm of smelly Bosun Squint ..."

You don't 'ave ter worry about yer fingers droppin' off Cap'n.

How so Squint?

'Cos I 'ad a bit of a wash this mornin'.

A bit of a wash!! And how did you manage this miracle?

I fell in a puddle!!

A puddle Squint!

Aye Cap'n. **A big one**, just outside the Dockyard gates!

Ye Gods! Falling into a filthy puddle doesn't count as **a bit of a wash!** ...

...although in your case, **it probably does!**

Thankee Cap'n... 'Twere a **clean puddle**.

Even so, methinks t'would be **safer** if you open the signal!

As you wish Cap'n.

Oh Lord, let it be a shore posting! **I'm sick of being sea-sick!**

... for fear he might get lost!

And so they gave him the very simple task of patrolling the Solent and the Isle of Wight (a task which required little or no navigational skill on Dyllbert's part provided he could keep the mainland in sight!), as a first line of defence against a possible, (but improbable) invasion by the French.

Still suffering with seasickness and unhappy with this (boring) role, Dyllbert continued to send signals (now marked urgent) to the Admiralty requesting a shore post, completely unaware that Lord Byron

Pudd, Flag Officer Prototype Ships has other plans for him.

Believing Dyllbert to be the most expendable officer in the Royal Navy, Pudd chooses him to command the sea trials of the Navy's latest top secret warship (and Admiral Nelson's intended Flagship).

Undoubtedly the greatest sea going weapon of the age, it is a paddle steamer with sails, (invented by the steam engineer Silas Smutt) which comes complete with a highly dangerous, untested and potentially explosive steam engine.

Of course, the treacherous Lord Pudd's plans are destined to completely backfire and, inevitably, he lives to regret choosing Dyllbert as his 'expendable' Captain.

Particularly so, as it is Pudd's actions, and Pudd's actions alone that eventually set Dyllbert on the path of historic destiny and of course finally, on to ...

THE ROAD TO PIRACY!

The Legend of Dyllbert the Pirate

"Dyllbert is about to read a signal from Lord Pudd. A signal that is to lead him to his destiny! ..."

PORTSMOUTH DOCKYARD

Right Squint, hold the signal steady ...

... Hmmm. It says I must report to Lord Pudd in London **immediately** ...

... **and tell no-one**, especially that smelly blabbermouth, Bosun Squint....**OH BLAST!**

Um, did you **hear** what I read Squint?

Aye Cap'n!

Then 'tis a terrible thing I must do to stop you blabbing!

Oh no Cap'n! You don't mean ...

Yes Squint! I must take your (sob) **smelly body** with me to London.

PHEW!! I feared you was a-gonna 'ang me!

Now there's a thought! However, there might be another way!!

OOH 'ECK!!

Character Profile

Bosun Squint

Bosun Squint, was born in Portsmouth, circa unknown. A foundling, he was adopted by Ollie and Mollie Squint, a family of self-employed cess pit cleaners.

Eventually press ganged into the Royal Navy (by an officer with a dreadful cold), Squint took to it like a duck to water. An excellent and brave sailor, (and despite his awful pong) he rose to the rank of Bosun in a very short space of time.

Naturally, because of his upbringing (and his aversion to washing), Squint fast became known as the smelliest sailor in the world and so was invariably swiftly transferred from ship to ship until, inevitably, he was assigned as Dyllbert's permanent Bosun.

Although at first, the bane of Dyllbert's life, Squint finally becomes his friend and indispensible right hand man.

Also a hopeless blabbermouth, Squint finds it next to impossible to keep a secret. He is, nonetheless, an extremely loveable character who eventually finds true happiness when he falls in love and marries a Tahitian Princess, who has no sense of smell!

The Legend of Dyllbert the Pirate

"Dyllbert and Squint are at the Globe Inn coach house in Oyster Street waiting to depart to London...."

T'is amazing how a **wodge of cotton wool** can dispel your **odious** smell, Squint!

What a pong!!

Ignore him Squint. Now, **you do understand the travelling arrangements?**

Aye Cap'n. But my legs ain't what they used to be!

Oh worry not Bosun. Your legs will keep up with the coach.

The London coach be leavin' in five minutes, will all those goin' kindly get a shift on. **Thankee!!**

Fear not everyone, **the Bosun will be travelling outside the coach!!**

Y I P P E E E E E E !!!

ZOOM

But 'ow can you be sure I won't fall be'ind Cap'n?

Because Squint, I have formulated a **foolproof plan!!**

The ☙ News

Newspapers in 1804, although printed and structured differently, were (oddly enough), very similar in content to todays newspapers.

The Portsmouth Telegraph or Mottley's Naval and Military Journal, an early local forerunner to The News, reported on Naval & Military battles, local news, theatre guides, events, crimes, adverts, jobs, houses for sale and ... lottery results.

Yes, there really was a State Lottery running in 1804 with a top prize of £30,000. And the cost of the Portsmouth Telegraph in Nelson's day? With an average wage of roughly 2 - 3 shillings (10 - 15p) per week, a pretty costly 6d (2½p).

Which just goes to prove that 193 years on, The News really is great value for money.

All the news that is the news is in

The ☙ News

Don't miss it!

27

The Legend of Dyllbert the Pirate

"Captain Dyllbert is preparing Squint, his smelly Bosun, for their journey to Admiralty House in London...."

This remarkable and unique establishment, which is situated in Queen Street, Portsmouth, was founded originally as a refuge for lower deck personnel of the Royal Navy in 1851 by well meaning local citizens who were appalled at the way a sailor was 'fleeced' of his meagre pay, by unscrupulous landlords, upon his return home after serving two to three years at sea.

Basically, the function of this, non profit making, club was to provide the poor sailor (for, in those days, poor he was) with inexpensive accomodation, food & drink. A place for the sailor to safely lay his weary head.

From 1917 to 1936, King George VI (then the Duke of York) was the President of the Royal Sailors Home Club and Patron from 1937.

In 1941, the original building was destroyed by enemy action, but by 1952, the first part of rebuilding the RSHC was completed and the second part by 1956. A families annexe of 3 floors was added in 1962 followed by an additional floor in 1968.

Today this extraordinary club continues to fulfill the purpose for which it was originally built. And many a sailor (then, as now) is thankful for it!

The Legend of Dyllbert the Pirate

"As Dyllbert and Squint travel to London, the *pressed crew* who are to trial Smutt's steamship have been assembled in ...."

PORTSMOUTH DOCKYARD

Right Private! Remove them there **shackles!**

Righto Sarge!

Now then. When I shouts yer name, you is to board that there vessel, **SHARPISH!!** ...

... GORDON BLUR Ship's Cook duties...

Aye!

... ANGUS McTICKLE First Mate duties...

Och Aye!

... GEORGE ABLEBODY Second Mate duties...

Duh, yup!

...WILLIE DIGGITT Chief Stoker duties.

Me! Chief Stoker! Oooer!!

What's a **Chief Stoker** Sergeant, bach?

No idea Diggitt! Best asks Mr Smutt. He'll know.

Dyllbert the Pirate's Fact File

Press Gangs

Probably the most feared and hated naval body of the 19th Century, the Press Gang comprised an officer backed up by several well trained and oft times ruthless and violent seamen and marines.

Originally, their job was to simply scour the streets and inns of coastal Towns just rounding up the volunteers or allocated men, and no more than that.

However, the truth of it is, when the Press Gang hit Town, any able bodied man was fair game. It mattered not if the poor man had just married or if he had a wife and children to support. If he was fit and able, he would be pressed into Naval service!

It is well known that pressed men cursed their fate and hated the service and were often among the most mutinous. In fact, the most notorious of the Spithead mutineers of 1797 were all pressed men.

Understandable when it is considered that all these sad, unfortunate men had to look forward to was brutal treatment, abject misery and literally years of separation from their loved ones.

However, some pressed men learned to enjoy the service and so volunteered to become proper naval ratings. The most notable being Lt. J. Quilliam, the first Lieutenant of HMS Victory who later became a Captain for his part in the Battle of Trafalgar!

The Legend of Dyllbert the Pirate

"With the volunteer crew safely aboard, Marine Sergeant Potty instructs his guards observed by a Dockyard pussy cat called *Weevil* ..."

Right you 'orrible 'erks! No-one boards that vessel wivout orders ter do so ...

... not even this friendly little pussy cat ...

... DO I MAKE MYSELF CLEAR!!!

Yes Sergeant!!

Now now pussy cat. You 'eard what the Sergeant said ....

.... you ain't allowed on that there boat! So **'OPPIT!!**

THUD

RETREAT!!

GRRRR !!

ARGHH! It's vicious!!

Coo, what a .... friendly .... (ouch) little .... pussy cat!!!

Blurgghh!!

Character Profile

Weevil The Dockyard Cat

Weevil is the most feared and hated cat in Portsmouth Dockyard. She is afraid of nothing or no-one and will happily attack, with her razor sharp claws, anything that dares to move!

In fact, when Weevil passes by, no-one who knows her has the courage to twitch, twiddle or move!

She is the undisputed Queen of the Dockyard but, like most cats, is also very curious and pompously investigates anything that takes her fancy.

And woe betide anyone who tries to stop her for, where Weevil wants to go, Weevil will go!

Based on a real Dockyard cat, Weevil eventually turns out to be a useful addition to Dyllbert's crew.

Weevil is also being produced as a beautiful soft toy and will be available in the shops in 1998. Watch the local press for details!

GRRR

The Legend of Dyllbert the Pirate

"Willie Diggitt seeks out Silas Smutt as *Weevil*, the fearsome Portsmouth Dockyard cat, sneaks aboard unseen ..."

Mr Silas Smutt. Are you there boyo? ...

LEAP

...Haloo Mr Smutt!!

Yes, I am here. Who calls?

Willie Diggitt. Ex-Welsh coal miner, recently pressed into Naval Service.

Pressed! How unfortunate Mr Diggitt ...

COAL

.... no doubt you'll miss being a coal miner!

Not me boyo! 'Cos ....

.... I really 'ated shovellin' that 'orrible filthy coal see!

Indeed, and what is your ship's duty Mr Diggitt?

BANG

Oh, **Chief Stoker**. Whatever that means?

Chief Stoker!! Oh dear. Well I fear it means you'll be, um ...

SLAM

SHOVELLIN' COAL BOYO!!! OH NO - O - O - O - O !!!

Dyllbert the Pirate's Fact File

Dockyard Cats

If it wasn't for the introduction of Cats into the Dockyards of England, it is quite likely that, by now, those very Dockyards would be completely overrun by disease carrying rats and mice. So, by keeping down the rodent population, the Dockyard cat certainly provides an essential service.

The true Dockyard cat is, in essence, as wild and as ferocious as its African cousin the Lion and, if taunted or intimidated will attack without hesitation.

However, although extremely cautious and wary of strangers, Dockyard cats will adopt and take titbits from the familiar hand of a friendly Dockyardman and will even allow a certain amount of petting. Weevil, our fictional Dockyard cat, is actually based on, and is a tribute to, a real cat who was involved in a terrible accident with a Dockyard Train.

Despite her back legs and tail being amputated by the wheels of the train, this truly spirited Portsmouth Dockyard wildcat continued to hiss and to claw at her human helpers, including a Dockyard Policeman, who gently comforted her until the vet arrived.

Sadly the vet could do nothing for her and so had no choice but to put her down. Even so, she refused to go quietly and her final act, in fine Dockyard wildcat tradition, was to sink her teeth into the unfortunate Policeman's thumb!

The Legend of Dyllbert the Pirate

"Unaware of the goings on in Portsmouth, Dyllbert meets with Lord Pudd who is angry with him for bringing the whiffy Bosun Squint ..."

What's that smelly blabbermouth doing here Dyllbert?

Er, he got wind of your secret signal sir.

He what!! Oddsbods!! **Where's the nearest yardarm?**

Hold sir. **You cannot hang Squint!** 'Twas my fault he heard me reading the signal.

EEK!!

He heard you!! Oh joy, I can hang him for **earwigging!!!**

But the blame is mine sir!

I don't care Dyllbert!! I just want to **hang the smelly swab!!**

I protest sir!!

(Sigh) Oh very well Dyllbert. I'll not hang him, this time! ...PROD!

You called sir?

Yes Prod. Get me a great big wodge of **cotton wool!!**

Right Dyllbert. Now Squint **can't earwig**, I shall explain everything!

Character Profile

Lord Byron Pudd
F.O.P.S.

Admiral Lord Byron Pudd is the Flag Officer Prototype Ships (F.O.P.S.) of the Admiralty in London and is the offspring of the late Lord Bertram and Lady Elizabeth Pudd.

Born circa 1745 at the Pudds Country Seat (Pudd House, near Wickham), with the proverbial silver spoon in his mouth, he is an arrogant and oft times overbearing man. He has however earned his Admiral's rank, serving with distinction aboard many Naval vessels and is a truly brave man who fears no-one. (No-one except his extremely sharp tongued wife, Lady Mildred Pudd that is!)

He has fought in numerous sea battles, and is friend to many Naval high rankers including of course, the heroic Admiral Lord Nelson.

He has also had the dubious pleasure (during the famous Spithead Mutiny of 1797) of serving aboard the same ship as the world's smelliest sailor, Bosun Squint, and knows well his revolting whiff and blabbing mouth.

Not known for making errors of judgement, he does nonetheless make a huge mistake in choosing Dyllbert as an 'expendable' Captain!

The Legend of Dyllbert the Pirate

"With his conk stuffed with cotton wool and Squint's hearing disabled, Pudd has explained the reason he needed to see Dyllbert so urgently ..."

So you want **me** to trial a **prototype steamship** sir?

Yes Dyllbert. What d'you think?

I think I'd like a **shore posting** sir!

Oh, that's out of the question Dyllbert.

How so sir?

Because, **I want you** to sea trial Smutt's steamship!!

Oh, that's out of the question sir!

How so Dyllbert?

Because, **I'm not going to do it!!**

WHAT!! Why you mutinous dog Dyllbert ...

... I'll have you thrown into the Tower of London!!!

Oh but sir!

... I thought you said a **shore posting** was **out of the question!!**

GGGGRRRNNFF!!!

Dyllbert the Pirate's Fact File

A Steamship in 1804?... Impossible!

"Of course it's impossible isn't it? Steamships weren't around until the 1830's, were they?" Well um... they were, actually! In fact, Steamship's began to appear at least a hundred years earlier.

In 1736, British engineer Jonathon Hull built a stern wheeler tugboat powered by British inventor Thomas Newcomen's atmospheric steam engine.

In 1783, Frenchman, Marquis Claude Francois de Jouffroy d'Abbans, built a steam powered paddle wheel boat called the 'Pyroscaphe' which puffed up the Saone river, near Lyon for 15 minutes.

In 1789, John Fitch and a German, Johaan Voight, went upstream on the Delaware river in a boat worked by 12 steam driven oars.

And, in 1802, Scotsman William Symington built a steamship called the 'Charlotte Dundas' which successfully towed two 70 tonne barges 19 miles in 6 hours against strong winds along the Forth-Clyde canal.

So, as can be seen, it was not impossible at all for steamships to be around in 1804. Which means that perhaps an inventor by the name of Silas Smutt really did invent a top secret, steam driven warship powered by paddle wheels and sails for Admiral Lord Nelson.

Then again... perhaps he didn't!

The Legend of Dyllbert the Pirate

"Dyllbert has refused to test Smutt's steamship. Lord Pudd is now a very desperate man ..."

Oh **please** test Smutt's steamship.

We-el, I will sir. But only on condition that ...

... I get a **shore posting** directly after the sea trials!

Oh, is that all!

Er, no sir. 'Twould have to be a **permanent posting.**

P-permanent!!

Yes sir. And in my home town of **Portsmouth!!**

Oddsbods! you drive a hard bargain ...

... (sigh) still, I will agree to your terms.

You will sir!!

Yes Dyllbert, you will have a **permanent** post in **Portsmouth** ...

Why thank you Lord Pudd.

... or at the bottom of the Solent if Smutt's steamship blows up!!

34

The Legend of Dyllbert the Pirate

"Having recruited Dyllbert as his expendable Captain, Lord Pudd turns to a more personal matter ..."

LORD BYRON PUDD F.O.P.S.

PROD! BRING YOUR SIGNAL PAD!!!

Aye aye sir!

Right Prod. Make to Portsmouth, "Smutt's ship to be named, er ...

... (Ahem) **THE BYRON PUDD!"**

The Byron Pudd! (grovel) Oh m'Lord. What an **honour.**

SIGNAL TO PORTSM SMUT TO BE

Indeed Prod!! Bestowed upon me by the new First Sea Lord, Henry Lord Melville himself!! ...

... Now, have it sent via the Shutter Telegraph **immediately!**

Aye aye sir.

This signal **must** be sent **without delay,** Lt. Tarbucket!

Well, I'll try Lt. Prod, **but I can't promise.**

SPIKE

Why, **what's the problem?**

It's just a **teensy bit foggy** today!!!

Character Profile

Lieutenant Prod

Lieutenant Prod is Admiral Lord Byron Pudd's devoted (and boot licking) secretary.

Born in Cosham circa 1770, of middle class parents, Prod despises (but secretly envies) Dyllbert.

He is without doubt a creep. A pompous and untrustworthy officer who considers anyone of equal rank or below to be way beneath his station in life.

Incredibly ambitious (but cowardly), he has a ready, and pretty sarcastic wit, which he uses at any and every opportunity to belittle, and score points off his fellow officers in front of Lord Pudd (or indeed any high ranking officer), in the hope of furthering his career.

Apart from Lord Pudd, he dislikes everyone and takes pleasure in others misfortunes.

There is however one person he would never dare belittle or attempt to score points off. And that person is ... Lady Mildred Pudd!

The Legend of Dyllbert the Pirate

"A signal from Lord Pudd is being sent from London to Portsmouth via the Admiralty's modern Shutter Telegraph System ..."

Foremastmen! Make to Portsmouth: "Smutt's ship to be named, **THE BYRON PUDD!!**"

Aye aye Lt. Tarbucket.

CHELSEA — PUTNEY HEATH — CABBAGE HILL

CLANK CLATTER

CLATTER CLANK

Message coming through the fog from London sir.

NETLEY HEATH — HASCOMBE — BLACKDOWN — BEACON HILL

CLANK CLATTER

CLATTER CLANK

Hurry midshipman, what is the message?

Well sir, this cloud keeps breaking up the signal but I think it's "**TO BE NAMED ... er, um???**"

And what is Smutt's ship to be called Midshipman Goodship?

Well sir ...

... I think it says: "**ER UM**"

Dyllbert the Pirate's Fact File

The Admiralty Shutter Telegraph System

In 1794 a Frenchman by the name of Claude Chappe invented and successfully installed a working T-type telegraph system at Belleville just outside Paris. It was the beginning of the communications revolution.

At that time, Britain was at war with France and had no communication device as sophisticated as Chappe's telegraph system. But, as luck would have it, a drawing of Chappe's design was found on the person of a French prisoner of war and so the Admiralty decided to rival it. But not precisely.

What they wanted was a simpler, cheaper device. What they ended up with was a remarkable system devised by Lord George Murray consisting of six shutters, all of the same square shape, which were moved by cranks, counterpoises and ropes.

Depending on position, each shutter represented a letter of the alphabet. The final version of Murray's system consisted of a two roomed hut comprising an operating room & living room/kitchen. On the roof was the 20ft high shutter telegraph assembly itself.

There were, finally, 64 such posts across Britain (including one on Southsea Common) linking the Admiralty in London to their coastal naval stations.

Although a crude device, the system was incredibly effective, it would take no more than 15 minutes for signals to travel from London to Portsmouth!

The Legend of Dyllbert the Pirate

"Lord Pudd's signal has arrived in Portsmouth Dockyard. Haplessly, due to foggy conditions, it's not quite the same signal he sent ..."

I say Mr. Plank! Where might I find your master, Mr. Smutt?

Well, you might find 'im in the engine room ...

... if (chuckle) 'e wasn't on the Isle 'o Wight a-visitin' 'is parents (titter).

Oh very funny!!

So, what did you want 'im for, Lieutenant?

I have an **urgent signal** for him from Lord Pudd ...

... regarding **the naming of his steamship.**

Best give me the signal then, cos ...

TAP TAP

... when Mr. Smutt's away, **I'm in charge!!**

Very well, see that the name is painted **without delay!!**

Don't you worry Lieutenant, **I'll paint the name on meself ...**

POKE

... It'll be an **'appy surprise** for Mr. Smutt when 'e gets back!

It won't be when he sees it!! (snigger)

Character Profile

Mr. Plank

Mr. Plank, born circa 1754 in Horndean, is the son of a Blacksmith and chief assistant to Silas Smutt (the inventor of the revolutionary steam engine and steamship destined to be Lord Nelson's Flagship).

Introduced to the skilled art of Smithying at a very early age, Plank learned much about the properties and the shaping of metal and iron.

But his heart wasn't really in it. His interest was in ships more than in Smithying and so (much to the disappointment of his dad), Plank entered into the trade of shipwright.

Chosen by Smutt to help in the construction of his steamship, Plank's former training as a Smithy soon proved to be of great value to Smutt.

And Smutt proved of great value to Plank too. For Plank discovered that he enjoyed working on Smutt's steam engine far more than working as a shipwright. And he was such a quick learner, Smutt actually trusted him to work alone at times!

Although a likeable fellow, Plank can become comically power crazy when given responsibility (as Chief Stoker Willie Diggitt eventually finds out).

The Legend of Dyllbert the Pirate

"Inventor Silas Smutt returns to Portsmouth Dockyard after visiting his parents in Cowes on the Isle of Wight ..."

Welcome back Mr. Smutt.

Thank you Mr. Plank. 'Tis good to be back.

I've a surprise for yer Mr. Smutt! Lord Pudd 'as chosen the name fer yer steamship!!

He has! Then pray reveal the name Mr. Plank.

Ooh, I can't do that Mr. Smutt. 'Twould spoil the surprise!!

Lawks! I wonder what deserved and heroic name has been chosen for my steamship!! ...

... The New Victory? Victory II? The Lord Nelson? Or ...

STAFF ENTRANCE

Aaarrrgggbbb!!!

The (sob) Iron flippin' Pudding!!!! (burble, sniff).

Bless 'im. He's all overcome with emotion!!

THE IRON PUDDING

Portsmouth
Flagship of Maritime England

Historic Ships, castles, forts and museums, spanning 800 years of history, burst into life when you visit Portsmouth.

Flagship Portsmouth, Portsmouth's historic dockyard, is a world class centre for Maritime Heritage. Explore Lord Nelson's HMS Victory, the world's first ironclad warship HMS Warrior 1860, Henry VIII's Mary Rose, and the Royal Naval Museum.

Other attractions include the D-Day Museum, Royal Marines Museum, Submarine World, Southsea Castle, City Museum, and overlooking the City, Fort Nelson.

The sea makes Portsmouth a great place to visit in other ways too. Just a stone's throw from the city centre is Southsea, a fully fledged seaside resort offering four miles of seaside fun. In Portsmouth Harbour, visit Port Solent, the largest marina development in north west Europe, with its impressive collection of shops and international restaurants.

Portsmouth is also the birthplace of a certain Charles Dickens, and there's a museum which commemorates this fact. Strangely enough, the city also has links with HG Wells, and Sir Arthur Conan Doyle. Indeed his most famous creation, Sherlock Holmes, was born here in 1886!

Portsmouth is also creating a multi-million dollar waterfront development to take it into the next millenium as the international tourist destination of Southern England.

Portsmouth Tourism, Civic Offices, Portsmouth, PO1 2BG Tel (01705) 834805 Fax (01705) 834975 Internet: http://www.resort-guide.co.uk/portsmouth

Portsmouth
FLAGSHIP CITY

The Legend of Dyllbert the Pirate

"Back at Admiralty House, Lord Pudd is about to receive some rather distressing news ..."

You asked me to remind you sir. Lady Pudd is visiting today.

Today! Oh Lor', I hope she's in a **good mood**!!

Oh, she will be **sir**, when she learns Smutt's ship has been **named after you.**

Beg pardon m'Lord. **A signal from Portsmouth.** I fear there's been **a mistake!**

A mistake Tarbucket?

Aye sir. They've named Smutt's ship, "**The Iron Pudding**"!!!

THEY'VE WHAT!!!...

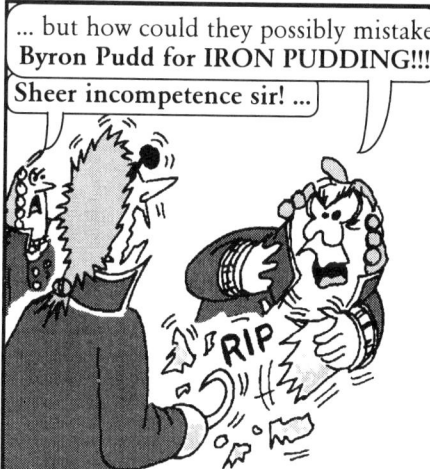

... but how could they possibly mistake **Byron Pudd for IRON PUDDING!!!**

Sheer incompetence sir! ...

...Heads will roll for this, Tarbucket, won't they m'Lord?

Oh yes Prod, **HEADS WILL ROLL!!**

(Gulp) **Including mine when M'Lady Mildred Pudd finds out!!**

The Legend of Dyllbert the Pirate

"The usually brave Lord Pudd is about to be visited by the one and only person he truly fears ..."

Er, Lady Pudd's carriage has arrived m'Lord!!

Oh Lor'!! Hide everything throwable!!

HURRY PROD!!

SMASH

Oh Lawks!

Well Byron! Has that **steamship** been named **after you?**

Er, well the thing is M-Mildred!! ...

...I f-fear there's been a b-bit of a m-mix up with the er, n-name. You see, er...

They've called it **THE IRON WHAT!!!**

Now c-calm yourself M-mildred!!!

I think she took the news **rather well**, don't you Prod?

Urrgghhh!!!

Character Profile

Lady Mildred Pudd

Lady Mildred Pudd (nee, Crabbit), the beloved wife of Lord Byron Pudd, secretly believes she is descended from Royalty. (Even though there is no actual proof that she is!)

However, being a veritably formidable lady (modesty forbids revealing her age) with a sometimes fearful temper and a tongue as sharp as a razor, no-one would dare argue that she isn't!

She certainly terrifies the life out of Lord Pudd and his boot-licking secretary, Lt. Prod, and is indisputably the ultimate snob.

An interfering and pushy lady, she revels in her position in life and enjoys reflecting in whatever glory her long suffering husband has, or is likely to achieve.

She is, nevertheless also a compassionate women who willingly does good works for charitable causes.

And woe betide anyone who doesn't agree to become involved, or attend any of her stupendously lavish fund raising events, Balls, or Galas!

The Legend of Dyllbert the Pirate

"Back in Portsmouth, having sent Squint to collect his belongings from *HMS Nauseas*, Dyllbert boards *The Iron Pudding* ..."

The Legend of
Dyllbert the Pirate

"Impressed with the luxurious *Iron Pudding*, Dyllbert now meets with his crew and explains their mission ..."

Right crew. 'Tis our task to **sea trial** this **fine ship**, which means ...

... we poodle around the Solent for three days and then return to Portsmouth ...

... whereupon you will doubtless be assigned to other ships of the fleet ...

GROAN!!!

... I am now going to issue you with a very essential piece of equipment. ...

...This equipment will defend and protect you during the course of our voyage!

But 'tis just a piece o' cotton wool Cap'n boyo!! What could cotton wool ...

... possibly protect us against?

Character Profile

Angus Mctickle
&
George Ablebody

Angus McTickle and George Ablebody are pressed men assigned to Smutt's Steamship, 'The Iron Pudding' as 1st and 2nd Mate's respectively.

The only reason they have been given their 'Mate' ranks however, is simply that, (having been regularly, albeit reluctantly, pressed into naval service on several occassions) they are considered 'experienced' sailors, which, as they have only ever been used for boarding party duties, they are not!

Angus McTickle hails from 'Glasgee' and is a proud Scot with an accent as thick as treacle.

Although slight of build, he has a fiery temper and is an expert with the cutlass.

George Ablebody on the other hand is a heavily built West Country man from Beer in Devon.

Considered 'slow brained' he is in fact, (at times) remarkably intelligent and clever. He has a soft melodic voice and, though extremely tough and very useful in a skirmish, has a heart as soft as butter.

Although 'chalk & cheese' they do become firm friends and eventually develop a total and unswerving loyalty to Dyllbert.

The Legend of Dyllbert the Pirate

"As *The Iron Pudding* is being prepared for her sea trials, Inventor Silas Smutt surprises his assistant, Mr. Plank ..."

I have decided that you shall be **the Engineer** for The Iron Pudding's trials Mr. Plank!

Me! Oh no Mr. Smutt ...

... 'Twas you wot designed 'er so **the honour must be yours.**

Oh pish Mr. Plank. **I must insist** it to be you **because** ...

... you have been a loyal assistant and trusted friend. **I must insist because** ...

... you have worked by my side, day by day with no complaints. **I must insist because** ...

ENGINE ROOM

... I think you truly deserve the honour of being The Iron Pudding's **First Engineer!!** ...

... and I must insist because I don't fancy being the one on board her if she blows up!!!

The Famous Folk of Portsmouth Town

Sir Arthur Conan Doyle (1859 - 1930)

Having obtained his MB in Edinburgh in 1881, the young Dr. Conan Doyle chose to establish a medical practice in Portsmouth and so took residence at No 1, Bush Villas, Elm Grove, Southsea in 1882.

By 1885, he had obtained his MD but, since he was already fairly engrossed with becoming a writer, his practice did not develop very rapidly at all.

It was, in fact, at Bush House that he wrote: 'A Study in Scarlet' which was the very first novel to feature his, now internationally renowned detective, Sherlock Holmes.

A little known fact is that Conan Doyle based Dr. Watson (Holmes great friend and biographer) on a Portsmouth man, namely: James Watson, a close friend, fellow doctor and member of the

Portsmouth Literary and Scientific Society (of which Conan Doyle was secretary).

Also a keen sportsman, Conan Doyle eventually became Captain of Portsmouth Cricket Club and also helped to found Portsmouth Football Club.

However, after eight very happy years, he decided to leave Portsmouth in 1890 for the sole purpose of advancing his medical career.

But, just one year later, (happily for us, and Sherlock Holmes) he finally abandoned the medical profession in favour of a distinguished literary career.

The Legend of Dyllbert the Pirate

"Meanwhile, back at Admiralty House in London, Lord Pudd is about to send another signal to Portsmouth via the Shutter Telegraph system ..."

Send that signal to Mr Smutt **immediately** Prod.

Aye aye sir.

Get this signal off to Portsmouth Dockyard forthwith, Tarbucket. Oh, and **try to get it right this time!!**

Oh, ha - flippin' - ha!

SPIKE

CLATTER CLANK

Message from the Admiralty sir, for a Mr. Smutt in Portsmouth Dockyard.

CLATTER CLANK

Very good Midshipman Goodship, make ready to send.

Ave aye sir.

PORTSMOUTH DOCKYARD

Beg pardon Mr. Smutt. A signal from Lord Pudd.

Thank you Lieutenant.

Lord and Lady Pudd arriving in Portsmouth tomorrow noon. Will meet you, four of the clock prompt, at George Hotel. Be sure you have a blasted good wash before we meet!!
Lord Pudd

RADIO Victory
95.6 FM CABLE & TV CHANNELS

In May 1994, after a break of almost a decade, Radio Victory made a nostalgic and welcome voyage back to the radio wavebands of Portsmouth (initially for a mere 28 days) to celebrate the Flagship City of Maritime England's historic 800th birthday and to commemerate the 50th Anniversary of D Day.

But, so successful was this voyage, Radio Victory returned permanently to her berth in Portsmouth and, for the past 3 years, has sailed along the airwaves of the Solent via the latest 'fibre optic' currents of Cable Television (Ch.42), fully committed to serving the community as only a truly Local Radio Station can!

Now, new horizons beckon as this much loved local radio station prepares to weigh anchor and set sail on a voyage of discovery, chasing the trade winds that will lead to a full time FM Broadcast license.

With a seasoned and dedicated crew, Radio Victory promises to faithfully serve the community by consistently delivering its rich and varied treasure of truly local news; great music; information and superb entertainment. But, above all, unlike other stations...

Radio Victory promises to remain Your Voice in the Community!

45

The Legend of Dyllbert the Pirate

"Mindful of Lord Pudd's signal, Smutt visits the bath house for a good scrub before his appointment with Pudd at the George Hotel ..."

BATH HOUSE - Bath Square

Return for me in one hour lads ....

La-de-da-de-da-de-day, scrub, scrub, scrub that muck away ...

... dum-de-dum-de-dum-de-da.

ONE HOUR LATER

To the George Hotel lads and **don't spare your legs!!**

GEORGE HOTEL

Ah, m'Lord Pudd. 'Tis a pleasure to see you again.

Hells teeth Mr. Smutt! I thought I told you to wash!!

Oh, b-but I have m-m'Lord!!

You have! Then oddsbods and buckets of tar, Mr. Smutt ...

... do you **have a problem!!!**

Aarrgghhh! It hasn't come off!!

Dyllbert the Pirate's Fact File

The George Hotel, High St. Portsmouth

On the morning of September 14th 1805, in the George Hotel, Admiral Nelson ate his last breakfast on British soil before joining his Flagship 'Victory' and sailing to his final 'death and glory' battle at Trafalgar.

After breakfasting, Nelson noted a crowd had gathered at the front of the George and, desiring to leave without fuss, left the Hotel by the rear entrance which led onto Penny Street.

But the crowd were not to be outdone and soon caught up with him on Southsea Common struggling with each other to shake the hand of their hero.

Nelson was overwhelmed by this and said "I wish I had two hands, then I could accomodate more of you". He then embarked from Southsea beach with the cries of "God bless you Nelson" ringing in his ears.

The origins of this once fine hotel can be traced back to the reign of King James the First when it was nothing more than a tiny thatched house with a water trough in front of it.

At that time it was know as 'The Wagon and Lamb' but, as the years passed by so this tiny house began to grow, both in size and importance. Re-named the George Hotel, it reached its peak in the 18th c.

The favourite watering hole of many famous naval heroes including: Collingwood, Hood, and Howe, it was sadly destroyed by German bombs in 1941.

The Legend of Dyllbert the Pirate

"The time has at last come for *The Iron Pudding* to begin her sea-trials. Mr. Smutt gives Dyllbert some last minute instructions ..."

Now remember Captain, 'tis most important **you do not fire up The Iron Pudding's engine** ...

... until you are **well clear** of the jetty. **And I mean well clear!!**

As you wish Mr. Smutt.

In fact, it might be better to wait until you've **cleared Portsmouth Harbour!**

Lawks, but you're nervy Mr. Smutt ...

... if I knew not better, I would be inclined to think (snigger) that ...

... you fear to start the engine close to the jetty (titter) just in case (giggle) ...

... the engine (chuckle) **explodes** and **blows everyone** (chortle) **to pieces!!!**

Got it in one Captain!!!

In the latter part of the 17th Century, Portsmouth Dockyard was expanding rapidly and so, in order to accommodate the much needed and ever increasing workforce, houses were built just outside the Dockyard ramparts, in what is today known as: 'Queen Street' and 'The Hard'.

Naturally, public houses were in greater demand than ever and it soon became very profitable for people to turn their homes into 'Ale Houses'. And so it was, in the early 18th Century, that the house known as; number 10, Common Hard, became 'The Ship Anson' under the proprietorship of: Joseph Scarrot.

Of course, The Ship Anson (now one of the oldest surviving pubs of that 18th Century period) has moved on somewhat since those early days.

Although proudly retaining its historic facade and interior, The Ship Anson is today a modern, friendly and congenial Family Pub where children are openly welcomed and excellent home cooked fare is offered in a wonderfully warm, convivial and inviting atmosphere. Why not come and see for yourself!

The Ship Anson - 10, The Hard, Portsmouth.
Telephone: 01705 - 838108

The Legend of Dyllbert the Pirate

"Before leaving *The Iron Pudding* and going ashore, Silas Smutt visits his assistant, Mr. Plank, in the engine room ..."

Well Mr. Plank, I wish you all good luck for the trials!

Thankee kindly Mr. Smutt! And may I say 'ow proud I am...

... that you chose me ter be **The Iron Puddin's** first engineer!

Oh, think nothing of it. 'Twas my pleasure. And now...

... I really must take my leave and go ashore.

Righto, Mr. Smutt. An' don't worry about yer engine. I'm sure it'll be fine!

Oh, I won't worry about my engine because when you fire it up ...

ENG ROO

... I'll be watching safely from shore!!

ABLEBODY!!!

Duh... Aye Cap'n?

THWACK!

Arggh!!

Cover that hatch afore someone falls down it!

Aye Aye, Cap'n!

URGGH!!

Character Profile

H.M.S. The Iron Pudding

"The Iron Pudding" is a prototype paddle steamer with sails and a flat bottomed hull which allows her to negotiate shallow waters quite easily.

Modified and adapted from a captured French, three masted frigate (the French built better warships than the British) in Portsmouth Dockyard, she is the brainchild of Engineer-inventor, Silas Smutt.

For the period (1804), she would undoubtedly have been the swiftest and most easily manoeuvrable Royal Naval warship in the world.

Destined to be Admiral Lord Nelson's new Flagship (in place of HMS Victory), she was originally to be named: "The Byron Pudd" after Lord Byron Pudd, the Flag Officer Prototype Ships.

Unfortunately, the signal, sent by shutter telegraph from Admiralty House London to HM Dockyard Portsmouth became confused, hence: "The Iron Pudding".

The Legend of Dyllbert the Pirate

"Under sail power, *The Iron Pudding* enters the Solent and Dyllbert discovers he has a rather reluctant stowaway ..."

Beg pardon Cap'n but Mr. Smutt be still aboard! 'E got knocked cold into the 'old!

Good Heavens!

Lawks Mr. Smutt! Are you alright?

Apart from a slight headache methinks! But that will pass once **I am ashore!**

Er, methinks 'twould **not be wise to go ashore right now** Mr. Smutt.

Huh, well methinks it would!

Aaarrrgghh! Where's the gangplank!!

Urgh! Come to that! Where's the perishin' dock!!

Well, I suppose I should really swim to shore now! And I would ...

SPLASH

...if I could (gurgle) ...

...flippin' well ...

glug glug

... swim. HELP!!!

The Famous Folk of Portsmouth Town

Herbert George (H.G.) Wells (1866 - 1946)

The son of a professional cricketer, HG Wells was born in Bromley on the 21st September 1866.

As a young man however, this distinguished writer of such classics as ' The War of the Worlds', 'The Invisible Man', and 'The Time Machine', lived in Southsea and was apprenticed to the drapers, Edwin Hyde (which, at that time, was situated on the corner of Kings Road and St. Pauls Road, Southsea).

But he despised the drapers trade (so much so, in fact, he recorded his experiences in his novel 'Kipps'), and so eventually forfeited his indentures and became a student teacher instead. From there he turned to writing and the rest, as they say, is history!

The Strange Tale Of Jeremiah Chubb

In a house in Daniel Street, Portsea, Jeremiah Chubb assembled and patented his revolutionary detector lock. 21 years later Jeremiah disappeared and drifted into poverty, whereupon his brother Charles first improved the lock, then founded the world famous firm of Chubb.

Jeremiah's last communication with his brother Charles was in 1839. Shortly after, with his wife and family, he vanished without trace and was never seen again! Just why he vanished still remains unsolved!

The Legend of Dyllbert the Pirate

"Having nearly drowned, Smutt finds himself back aboard *The Iron Pudding* pondering his fate ..."

(Sigh) Well Silas, 'tis just typical... **Saved from drowning** ...

... only to face being **blown to pieces** by your **own perishin' engine**! ...

... Ah well, 'tis obvious the fates have decreed that **I be on The Iron Pudding** ...

... and so if my engine blows up, **I will accept** that 'tis **my time to go** ...

... and I shall face my going with **grit, fortitude, dignity and** ...

PREPARE TO FIRE UP THE ENGINE MR. PLANK!

EEEK!!!

Waahhh!. Don't start the engine! *(sob).* I don't want to *(blubber)* d-d-die!!!

EH?

When Portsmouth became a fortified Town with ramparts, bastions, gates & drawbridges, a certain part of the Town, known as 'Point' was excluded.

This didn't really bother the inhabitants of 'Point' however, since they enjoyed a number of 'privileges' denied to those residing within the Town walls.

One particular (and presumably very popular) privilege, allowed licensed victuallers the right to keep their inns and pubs open all day and all night which meant, for many years, 'Point' was witness to nightly scenes of serious 'Bacchanalian' orgies.

'Point' was (and still is) also known as 'Spice Island' (apparently earning this nickname due to the icky whiff the lack of proper sanitation produced). Happily, those days are long gone and 'Spice Island' is now a genuinely beautiful & worthy place to visit.

Even more so for the truly traditional Family Tavern, the 'Spice Island Inn'. Open all day, every day it boasts fine harbour views, excellent bar snacks and a superb menu (including freshly caught local fish).

Spice Island Inn, Bath Square, Old Portsmouth.
Telephone: 01705 - 870543

The Legend of Dyllbert the Pirate

"Down in the engine room and still under orders to fire up the engine, Mr. Plank gives Willie Diggitt his orders ..."

Right then **Diggitt!** Open that **coal 'atch** and start **a-shovellin'**.

Grrr, I 'ate coal!

WATER

'Ere, 'old up Diggitt! That lump o' coal on the end o' yer shovel **jus' moved!**

COAL

(Gulp) **M-moved Mr. Plank!** *(twitter)* Are you sure?

I fink so!

And *(gulp)* 'as that lump o' coal **got eyes,** Mr. Plank?

Yeah! *(shiver)* **Girt big green ones!**

Then we're doomed boyo 'cos *(gulp)* that's the *(quake)* dreaded **green-eyed coalmine monster!**

C-coalmine monster! Ooh 'eck! Wot are we gonna do?

(Whisper) There's only one thing *(shake)* we can do Mr. Plank.

(Whisper) And wot's that Diggitt?

RU-U-U-NNNN!!!

ZOOMM

Character Profile

Willie Diggitt

Willie Diggitt, was born in Wales in 1775 in Llanfairpwllgwyngyllgogerychwyrndrobwllllantysiliogogoch (where else), and is an ex Welsh coal miner, (man and boy).

Sick to the back teeth with working in a dark pit, breathing in coal dust and, in particular, shovelling coal by the ton, Willie packed his meagre belongings (including his shovel, candle and candle holder), bade a tearful farewell to his ma and pa, and set off for London to seek his fortune.

However, things don't go exactly to plan.

For, upon his arrival in the 'Big Smoke', Willie is immediately press ganged into the Royal Navy.

Oddly enough, happy in the knowledge that at least he won't be shovelling any more of that hated coal anymore, Willie is happy with this turn of events and looks forward to a life at sea, sampling lungful's of good, clean, fresh sea air.

There is, however, a fly in Willie's ointment as he learns when assigned to "The Iron Pudding" as Chief Stoker and finds out that his main duty will be...

... shovelling coal by the ton!

The Legend of Dyllbert the Pirate

"Unaware of Diggitt's *coal monster*, Dyllbert questions Smutt about his reluctance to fire up his engine ..."

Explain yourself, Mr. Smutt!

Engine *(gibber)* **Don't fire up!** *(gabble)* **Might blow ...**

Aarrggh! Cap'n Dyllbert boyo! Save us!!

What on earth!

We're doomed Cap'n bach! There's a coalmine monster aboard!

Diggitt speaks true Cap'n! I seen it meself!

Aarrgghh! There it is!

Oh yes Diggitt! 'Tis a most fearsome *(giggle)* **"coalmine monster" pussy cat!!!**

Oh 'eck! That be not just a pussy cat Cap'n. That be evil Weevil...

.... the most vicious cat in Portsmouth Dockyard! She attacks anyfink wot moves!!!

GRRRR   HISS

(Gulp) Does she really Squint!!!

The Famous Folk of Portsmouth Town

King William The Fourth (1765 - 1837)

The Monarch (formerly known as 'Prince') was the third son of (mad) King George the Third, and was known as the 'Sailor King'. As a midshipman, the young Prince spent a good deal of his time in Portsmouth, and often stayed at the George Hotel in the High Street.

One of the most enduring tales of William's time in Portsmouth was when he became involved in a fight with a waterman after visiting a public house in Tower Street (adjacent to Broad Street near the Round Tower).

The cause of the fight was simply that the Prince had cheekily consumed the waterman's beer.
As a result, William (who the waterman believed was just a little 'snot-nosed' midshipman), was given a 'sound thrashing'.

However, on learning Prince William's true identity, the waterman's face paled, and he rightly feared that, having struck the King's son, he would, at best, be incarcerated in the Tower of London for the rest of his life or, at worst, be hung (painfully), drawn and, (agonizingly) quartered!

Instead, much to the waterman's surprise (and luck), he was heartily commended by the good Prince William and, (as a reward) was given a lucrative post in the Customs and Excise Department.

The Legend of Dyllbert the Pirate

"After days trapped in *The Iron Pudding's* engine room coal bunker, Weevil, the feared Portsmouth Dockyard cat is free ..."

(Whisper) Oh 'eck *(tremble)* Weevil's a-comin' this way Cap'n!

(Whisper) Yes Squint, *(gulp)* I know!

Oh lawks Squint! I can't see her! Where is she?

She's a-layin' down by yer feet Cap'n!!

Laying by my feet? Is that all?

Aye Cap'n.

Ye Gods. She's **starved!** Blurr, bring meat to my cabin. **She needs urgent feeding!**

Aye aye Cap'n!

Oh, and **Sergeant Potty**...

SAH!!!

... Put **Mr. Smutt** in irons then bring him to me! ...

EEEK!

.... He has a great deal of explaining to do!!

GIBBER!

Character Profile

Sergeant Potty & his Marines

As his name suggests, *Sergeant Potty is a bit 'potty'.*

An archetypal Sergeant, he has a mouth like a foghorn and a bullish manner.

Although obviously an illiterate dimwit (who is easily fooled into believing anything and everything his beloved Captain Dyllbert chooses to tell him), he is, nevertheless, a hugely loveable character as are the Marine Privates under his command, Arfur and Bert.

The Legend of Dyllbert the Pirate

"Dyllbert has taken the starving Weevil to his cabin to feed her. Meanwhile, Sergeant Potty escorts the arrested Smutt ..."

This is all **a terrible mistake Sergeant!**

That's as maybe sir! But **orders is orders!**

Beg pardon Cap'n, but I 'as brung Mr Smutt as per your order!

Very good Sergeant Potty. Show him in!

So Mr. Smutt! What's all this about **your engine?**

(Gulp) Well Captain, er... now **don't get angry** but, um...

LATER So! You and Lord Pudd **knew** your **engine might blow!**

T'was **Pudd** that chose you as his *expendable Captain*, not I ...

... Now might I suggest we return to **Portsmouth** and ...

Return to Portsmouth! Oh no Mr. Smutt! ...

... I am now **determined to trial** this ship, and your engine ...

GULP!

... and you, Mr. Smutt, are going to help me!!!

Me! Oh lawks!! (*swoon*)

The Famous Folk of Portsmouth Town

Charles Dickens (1812 - 1870)

Undoubtedly, the most famous locally born author and the most popular novelist of the 19th Century, Charles (Huffam) Dickens was born at 393 Commercial Road Portsmouth on the 7th February 1812 and was baptised at St. Mary's Church.

Four months after his birth, his family moved to poorer quarters in Hawke Street, Portsea where they resided for the next two years before going to London.

In 1824, the family fell upon hard times when his father was imprisoned for debt and the 12 year old Dickens had to work in a blacking factory.

However, determined to better himself, he worked extremely hard, taught himself shorthand writing and eventually became a reporter.

When his novel, 'The Pickwick Papers' was published in 1837, it brought him overnight fame and he never looked back.

He returned to the place of his birth in 1838, seeking inspiration for his book, 'Nicholas Nickleby' and unashamedly used parts of Portsmouth as a backdrop, having Nicholas & Smike entering the Town through the 'Landport Gate' and finding lodgings above a tobacconist's on the 'Common Hard'.

Portsmouth is rightly proud of this truly gifted man who gave a reading of his works in St. Georges Hall, Portsea in 1866, 4 years before his sad demise.

The Legend of Dyllbert the Pirate

"Smutt has confessed to Dyllbert that he and Lord Pudd knew his engine might explode. Dyllbert has formulated a plan of action ..."

Being a **fair Captain,** I have decided to give you **a choice!**

A choice Captain?

Yes Mr. Smutt. 'Tis **your choice** to either **start your engine ...**

... or swim to Portsmouth Dockyard!

URGH!

LATER

Right crew. Mr. Smutt has **bravely chosen** to start his potentially **explosive engine. ...**

... **His bravery** prompted me to tell him that **we would be fully behind him ...**

Altho' I must confess, I er, did not tell him exactly ...

... just how far behind him we would actually be!!!

Dyllbert the Pirate's Fact File

The Tale of the Captain's Furniture!

Prior to engaging the enemy in battle, warships were cleared for action. This meant moving and stowing away items that might otherwise hinder the action and performance of the ships crew.

This also applied to the Captain's cabin which had to be cleared of all his fine furniture (most of it personal), in order that cannons could be rolled in by the gun crews and be placed in position at the rear windows.

But once removed, where on earth could the crew safely stow their Captain's valuable furniture and save it from certain damage from cannon-fire?

Well, actually, they stowed it in a rowing boat!

And exactly where did they put this rowing boat stuffed full of their Captain's precious furniture?

Well, unbelievably, it was lowered over the side into the water and then towed behind the ship!

This apparently was the safest place for it, simply because of a gentlemen's agreement between opposing Captains that, whilst happy to blow each others ships out of the water, they would not, under any circumstances, fire upon the rowing boat that carried each others furniture!

This being the case, one must wonder just how many of the ship's crew bravely volunteered to sit in the rowing boat and look after the Captain's goods!

The Legend of Dyllbert the Pirate

"Smutt has successfully started *The Iron Pudding's* engine and Dyllbert wants to be the first to offer his hearty congratulations ..."

Well Mr Smutt. Your worries were **needless. Your engine works!!**

Hmph! *I* was never worried Captain!

However methinks 'tis time for **you to worry!**

Me? How so?

Because, unlike you, **I am of great importance to Lord Pudd,** and so....

... methinks 'tis certain you will **suffer his fearful wrath** ...

... if you don't release me and put me ashore **this very perishin' minute!**

Lawks! 'Twould seem I have no choice but to put you ashore! **And so I shall...**

Ha! The thought of Pudd's wrath has **scared him totally out of his wits!**

... the very perishin' minute I decide to flippin' well do so!!!

(Gulp) **Well perhaps not totally out of his wits then!!!**

The Famous Folk of Portsmouth Town

William Lionel Wyllie (1851 - 1931)

One of the most celebrated artists of modern times, William Wyllie lived in Tower House in Broad Street Portsmouth from where he painted many wonderful pictures depicting Navy life.

And, such was the standing of this remarkable marine artist, the Royal Navy actually afforded Wyllie a most unusual & unprecedented honour.

Upon his death, Wyllie's body was ceremoniously conveyed in a cutter of HMS Nelson up Portsmouth harbour to Portchester Castle.

As the cutter procession passed by, warships at anchor in the harbour silently dipped their colours in deference and in rememberance of Wyllie.

Upon reaching Portchester Castle, his body was ceremoniuously conveyed through the Roman Water Gate and then on to its final resting place, the picturesque churchyard of St. Mary's.

His last great (and some say his finest) work was that of the quite stupendous panoramic view of the Battle of Trafalgar.

This painting he very generously presented to the nation in honour of England's most distinguished naval hero, Admiral Lord Horatio Nelson.

This spectacular painting is on display, and can be viewed, in the Historic Dockyard Museum, Portsmouth.

The Legend of Dyllbert the Pirate

"*The Iron Pudding's* trials are going so well, Dyllbert has time to relax in his cabin and reflect on Lord Pudd's treachery ..."

So, Lord Pudd thought me **expendable** eh, Weevil! It must follow then that ...

... had Smutt's engine exploded, **my loss**, and the **loss of my crew**, would have mattered **not a jot!** ...

... Of course, 'tis obvious why he did not just ask for a volunteer! ...

'Twas because he knew that **any sensible Captain** would have rightly said...

... NOT ON YOUR FLIPPIN' NELLIE SQUIRE! ...

WAIL

... Well Weevil, I'll make M'Lord Pudd regret making me his *expendable Captain!* For at **two of the clock** ...

... the day after tomorrow, methinks he will wait a very long time for the return of his precious *Iron Pudding!*

THE IRON PUDDING

Dyllbert the Pirate's Fact File

The Pirates!

"In the mind of the mariner, there is a superstitious horror connected with the name of... 'Pirate', and there are few subjects that interest and excite the curiosity of mankind more than the desperate exploits, foul doings and diabolical careers of these monsters in human form ..."

So wrote Charles Ellms of Boston in "The Pirates Own Book" in 1837 and his words are as true today as they were then, for although Pirates are no longer seen as 'monsters', the very name; 'Pirate' still excites the curiosity and cannot help but conjure up the image of a romantic, mysterious yet threatening and fearful figure, a-roaming the seas in search of adventure, victims and ... treasure!

But how monstrous were these Pirates of old?

Were they really nothing more than a bunch of mindless, murderous, greedy and untrustworthy freebooters?

For the most part, they probably were. But, they were also expert seamen and navigators and, moreover, (according to Captain Charles Johnson who in 1724 published a book entitled: 'A general history of the robberies and murders of the most notorious Pirates') followed a strict Pirate code of conduct.

Continued overleaf ...

The Legend of Dyllbert the Pirate

"Having turned Pirate and secured the loyalty of his crew, Dyllbert's next task is to bring Sergeant Potty round to his way of thinking ..."

Back to your duties men and **speak naught** of our plans. **Squint, send Sergeant Potty to me!**

Aye aye Cap'n

Ah, Sergeant Potty. Do come in, I have something to tell you.

SAH!

I have, this very night, received **new orders** from the Admiralty saying, we are to **cease the trials forthwith** ...

... and **seek, harry and destroy** our enemies ships in the er, guise of um, **Pirates!**

PIRATES SAH!!! Good 'Eaven's above!

Now, as you are in charge of this ship's Marine contingent, 'tis your duty ...

... **to read and verify these orders.** Er, I assume you **can read** Sergeant Potty?

Read Sah? Oh yes Sah ...

... I can read alright!!

OH NO YOU CAN'T!!!

LUV

Dyllbert and Weevil

Pirates... Fact, Fiction And Myth

Piracy has been around for thousands of years and is not just a 'man thing'. Women too have been very successful Pirates.

One such woman was the female Chinese Pirate chief, 'Ching Shih', who commanded a fleet of 800 large junks and 1000 smaller vessels and who terrorised the China seas during the early 1800's. Mary Read and Anne Bonny were British Pirates who dressed as men and sailed with the infamous Pirate; Calico Jack, (John Rackham) in the 1700's.

There have been Greek, Danish, Viking and Roman Pirates. In fact in 286BC, the Romans sent a sea Captain called Carausius to Portsmouth in order to suppress piracy in the area. This turned out to be a bit of a mistake on Rome's part however, since Carausius became a Pirate himself!

Walking the plank is a myth. Pirates never made their victims, or each other, walk the plank.

The popular image of a Pirate Captain with eye patch, wooden leg and scruffy clothing is generally inaccurate. Many Pirates became extremely wealthy

and dressed accordingly. The Pirate Black Bart for example wore a crimson damask waistcoat and breeches, feathered hat and heavy jewellery.

Treasure maps and buried treasure, popularised in Robert Louis Stevenson's 'Treasure Island' hardly feature in true Pirate history. Most Pirates squandered their booty on gambling, women and heavy drinking.

Except it would seem for Captain Kidd who actually did bury his treasure ...

... somewhere on Gardners Island in the Pacific Ocean.

The Legend of Dyllbert the Pirate

"Gambling Potty can't read, Dyllbert has shown him a fictitious Admiralty Order saying they are to assume the guise of Pirates..."

HM Royal Dockyard Portsmouth

The Times Obituary Column
Monday 1st October 1984

"HM Royal Dockyard Portsmouth passed peacefully away at 12 o'clock last night after nearly 800 years of faithful service. It will be sadly missed by many."

Such was the depth of feeling at the passing of Britain's foremost Royal Dockyard, it was actually deemed worthy of this unique national tribute.

And quite naturally so too, for it was after all, the end of a quite stupendous era in British naval history, and the beginning of an exciting new one.

From that day forward, 'HM Royal Dockyard' officially became the 'Fleet Maintenance and Repair Organisation' and, although ships are no longer built there, the Dockyard continues to be a truly versatile ship repair base capable of all manner of tasks and justly proud of its 'we can do it' reputation.

Portsmouth Historic Dockyard

In 1985, the Portsmouth Naval Base Property Trust (a registered charity), was created to undertake the essential upkeep of the Historic Dockyard and the important preservation of its buildings and docks, thereby conserving Britain's truly exceptional naval heritage for the free pleasure, education and enjoyment of all.

Continued overleaf ...

The Legend of Dyllbert the Pirate

"Altho' Dyllbert easily convinced Sgt. Potty they are to disguise themselves as Pirates, Smutt is a different kettle of fish entirely ..."

I 'as brung Mr. Smutt as ordered Sah!

Very good Sergeant. Send him in then wait outside my cabin door.

Well Mr. Smutt, I have grave news to impart. **You see, the Admiralty ...**

LATER

They want you to act as Pirates! I don't believe it! Let me see the orders!

I fear you can't. I accidentally dropped them out of my cabin window!

Oh, how convenient! It can't be true because **The Iron Pudding** is to be ...

Hold Mr. Smutt! I almost forgot! Sergeant Potty can confirm the orders ...

... for he has read them personally!

Potty! Huh, I'll wager that illiterate oaf can't read for flippin' toffee!

GRRR!!!

SMASH

EEEK!

Oh dear, methinks he may have heard you Mr. Smutt!

Now you ain't a-castin' nasturtiums an' incineratin' I can't not read, is you Mr. Smutt?

Er, *(gulp)* nope!

... Within the walls of Portsmouth Historic Dockyard are treasures beyond price. Treasures that do not belong to any one organisation but to the entire British nation.

Treasures such as the ironclad 'Warrior', which in 1861 was simply the world's biggest, swiftest and most heavily armed and armoured warship. She was the ultimate deterrent and no-one, including France's Emperor Napoleon III, dared engage her.

And then there is the mighty 'Mary Rose' the pride of Henry VIII's fleet that after braving many sea battles was so tragically lost in the Solent.

And finally, the world's greatest and most enduring warship: Nelson's 'Victory'

It is easy to walk the decks of the 'Victory' where England's heroic Admiral Lord Nelson fell in the service of his country, and imagine just what it must have been like to have been aboard her in the heat of a terrible battle.

To sense the understandable, stomach churning fear of the fighting men. To almost smell the choking acrid smoke of cannon fire, to hear the shouted orders of officers and the terrible cries of the injured and dying, the crash of cannonball and the thunderous crack of splintering wood.

To know that on this ship (as on many others before her and after), here fought the best and most disciplined seamen in the world.

These ships are the pride of England. They are the immortal and abiding testaments to the truly courageous and indomitable 'Hearts of Oak' spirit of the British seamen, past and present.

God bless 'em all.

The Legend of Dyllbert the Pirate

"Having dealt with Smutt satisfactorily, a happy Dyllbert composes a letter to Lord Pudd. But not all are as happy as he ..."

WHO IS IT?

Gordon Blurr, the ship's cook Cap'n. Might I 'ave a word?

What can I do for you Blurr?

Well Cap'n. I've no desire to be a **Pirate cook**, so...

... I request that I be put ashore at your convenience!

Hm! Very well Blurr. I will agree to your request, provided ...

... you agree to deliver this message to Lord Pudd!

I will Cap'n. And **thankee** ...

... you are indeed a **good and fair man!**

SQUINT!

You called Cap'n?

Yes Squint. Set course for the **Isle of Wight!** We are to put Blurr ashore!

Oh, and Squint! You'll be **cooking tonight!**

Me! Ooer! I wonder if I should tell 'im I can't cook!

Character Profile

Gordon Blurr

Gordon Blurr was born in Southampton in 1765 the son of a candle-maker.

Originally pressed into Naval service, Blurr discovered that he actually enjoyed the life and therefore became a volunteer. He eventually rose to the rank of gunner's mate and the future looked rosy.

Sadly, during a sea battle, Blurr's right leg got in the way of an enemy cannonball and so it, and the rest of Blurr, parted company. Fitted with a wooden 'peg-leg', Blurr left the navy, cursing the service and blaming it for his tragic misfortune.

Blurr finds work in a Southampton hostelry as a cook and, it is whilst working there that he fell in love and married the owners daughter. Haplessly, shortly after the wedding, Blurr was reluctantly press ganged into becoming ship's cook aboard "The Iron Pudding".

Naturally all Blurr wants is to get back to the hostelry and his wife. Luckily for him, Dyllbert's decision to become a Pirate offers him the chance to do just that. However, that is not the last we shall see of Gordon Blurr, for he returns in Book 2 in ...

"The Capture of Cookie Le Crumble"

The Legend of Dyllbert the Pirate

"As dawn breaks and a lazy sun rises in the East, *The Iron Pudding* anchors off the coast of a mist shrouded Isle of Wight ..."

Right Blurr! Deliver this message to **Lord Pudd** on **Pitch House Jetty** ...

... in **Portsmouth Dockyard** this **very day**!

Aye aye Cap'n. I'll not let you down!

Squint! Row Blurr ashore, then pop into Ryde and purchase me ...

... a **Parrot** from a pet shop. After all, a **Pirate** without a **Parrot** is not a true **Pirate**!

Aye aye Cap'n!

HIGH ST. RYDE

Will yer stop makin' them **wheezin' noises** you **dozy Penguin**! Yer drivin' me **nuts**!

PET SHOP

WEEZE

Oh Lord! Please send me a **right berk** I c'n sell this **perishin' bird** to!

Mornin' shipmate!

DING!

Oh, thank you Lord!!!

WEEZE

Character Profile

'Arry the Asthmatic Penguin

'Arry the Asthmatic Penguin, is a cute, and instantly loveable baby penguin with a serious asthma problem who becomes the property of Dyllbert the Pirate.

Sold as an 'Arctic Parrot' to Bosun Squint by a pretty shrewd and astute Isle of Wight pet shop owner, poor little 'Arry suffers terribly from all numbers of allergies.

Happily, (in book 2: 'The Capture of Cookie Le Crumble) 'Arry does eventually receive help from Ships Doctor Esau Bones and Engineer Silas Smutt who invent a wierd and wonderful steam powered contraption that eases poor 'Arry's suffering.

It is hoped by the authors that 'Arry will be an educational aid to the story and will therefore go some way in highlighting the real life problems faced by asthma sufferers the world over.

'Arry is also being produced as a beautiful soft toy and will be available in the shops in 1998. Watch the local press for details!

The Legend of Dyllbert the Pirate

"Under orders from Dyllbert to purchase him a Parrot, Bosun Squint is in a pet shop in Ryde on the Isle of Wight ..."

So, 'tis **a Parrot** you wants, eh, matey?

No, not me! 'Tis me Cap'n wot wants one!

Oh, an' who might yer Cap'n be?

'E be (whisper) **Dyllbert the Pirate!**

Dyllbert the Pirate eh! Never 'eard of 'im!

Well that's 'cos **he's new!** 'E only started **Piratin' this mornin'!!**

A **new Pirate** eh! Well, he'll not be a-wantin' any o' these **scraggy ol' Parrot's** will 'e? ...

... No! He'll be a-wantin' an **extra special Parrot!** And as **luck** would 'ave it ...

... I've got the very fing in this 'ere cage! The **rarest Parrot in the World! I give you** ...

... 'Arry, the Arctic Parrot!!!

Coo!

WEEZE GASP WHISTLE

Character Profile

Dr. Esau Bones

Dr. Esau Bones, was born in 1752 in London and is the only son of the eminent surgeon: Dr. T.Bones.

Although, from an early age, his main interest was in ornithology, Bones followed in his Father's footsteps and studied medicine.

Naturally, this involved reading and studying medical books on ailments and diseases, which in turn led to Bones eventually developing acute hypochondria.

So much so in fact, he has (in his mind), so far contracted every known ailment and disease under the sun, including the plague!

Believing that a good sniff of the old briny might help to cure all his imaginary ills, Bones offers his medical and surgical skills to the Royal Navy.

Sadly, the Admiralty, who are not prepared to engage a hypochondriac as a ships doctor, turn him down.

Miffed, but undaunted, Bones decides to join a merchant ship and inevitably ends up on Dyllbert's pirate ship 'The Iron Pudding'. See him in 'The Legend of Dyllbert the Pirate', Book Two entitled ...

" The Capture of Cookie Le Crumble "

The Legend of Dyllbert the Pirate

"Squint has returned to the Iron Pudding with the *Arctic Parrot* he's purchased for Dyllbert ..."

'Tis an **odd looking Parrot,** Squint!

That's 'cos he's a **rare Arctic Parrot,** Cap'n!

WEEZE GASP

And why is he making that **wheezy** noise?

I expect it's 'cos 'e be 'appy, Cap'n!

WEEZE GASP

Yes of course! Well, let's have him out of the cage.

PURRR!!   *WHEEZE*

... and see **how well he sits upon my shoulder!**

Hm! Methinks he needs to **work on his balance,** Squint!

Oh, he'll get **the 'ang of it,**

So **Weevil,** my furry little friend. What think you of **'Arry, the Arctic Parrot!!**

PURR PURR!!!

In future episodes in the 'Legend of Dyllbert the Pirate' Cartoon Book Series, you will meet ...

Capitaine Henri LeTeef & Lt. Jean Pierre LeTwerp

Capitaine Henri LeTeef is a French Privateer in the pay of Napoleon Bonaparte who has the constant misfortune of coming into conflict with Dyllbert the Pirate, time after time ... after time!

He is however a brave, determined and fiercely loyal Frenchman who obsessively (and some might say, foolishly) chases after, and has sworn to capture, Dyllbert and 'The Iron Pudding' at all costs (fat chance).

LeTeef's loyal, but comical, second in command is Lt. Jean Pierre LeTwerp. Although also a brave and allegiant Frenchman, his loyalty to LeTeef is sometimes tested beyond endurance by his Capitaine's obsession with capturing Dyllbert!

The Legend of Dyllbert the Pirate

"Having turned Pirate, Dyllbert knows he must now flee the Solent and the inevitable vengeful anger of Lord Byron Pudd ..."

Right Squint! Weigh anchor and **put distance between us and Portsmouth!**

And **wot course** be we takin Cap'n?

C-Course! *(Gulp)* Oh er, Good point Squint! I'll check my charts and um, **plot us one!!**

(Sigh) **I never could grasp the basics of navigation!** Can't let the crew know!!

Now, if that's **longitude** ... then this must be **latitude** ... or *(gulp)* **is it the other way round!**

Phew! I've done it. Navigation isn't that difficult after all!! In fact, **pretty simple really!!!**

Squint! You can weigh anchor! I've plotted our course!

Aye aye Cap'n. **Wot be our course then?**

Er well, *(blush)*, **straight ahead, turn left at Dover and up the right hand side of England!**

?

Mr. Riddles (Aka: Mr. Smith the Spy)

Mr. Riddles is a rather arrogant freelance news reporter for the 'Portsmouth Telegraph' who has no scruples and will therefore report on anything regardless of National Security....

Because of this, Riddles eventually falls foul of Lord Byron Pudd (discovering that Pudd is the very last person to cross). And just how exactly does Mr. Riddles become 'Smith the Spy'? Well, all will be revealed in future episodes where you will also meet...

Mrs. Millicent Dyllbert

Dyllbert's widowed, short sighted and hard of hearing mum.

She is a really sweet little lady who, owing to her hearing problems, invariably mis-hears words. This of course results in her getting a wee bit confused. She eventually ends up on 'The Iron Pudding' with her son (she knits him a sail for his birthday) where she causes unintentional havoc!

Fairface Teach (the Pirate)

A descendant of the infamous Edward Teach (Blackbeard the Pirate).

The beautiful Fairface Teach is a fierce, brave and formidable female Pirate Captain who, with her all female crew, is currently the scourge of the seven seas.

Although her present ship, 'The Bounteous' is a superb vessel, Fairface desires only the best and is therefore determined to capture 'The Iron Pudding' (by fair means or foul) and make it her own ...

The Legend of Dyllbert the Pirate

"As Dyllbert heads up the right hand side of England, Lords Pudd, Nelson and Melville wait in vain the return of *The Iron Pudding ...*"

PITCH HOUSE JETTY

Oddsbods Horatio! **The Iron Pudding** should have arrived by now!

Yes. I wonder why she hasn't?

Huh, **Dyllbert's useless navigation** probably!!

Doubtless you are right **Lord Melville**, still...

LORD PUDD ... LORD PUDD!!!

Prod! What the devil!!!

This is **Gordon Blurr, The Iron Pudding's** cook m'Lord!

Iron Pudding's cook! Then why are you not aboard her, Mr. Blurr?

The Captain of The Iron Pudding sent me to deliver this message to you m'Lord!

Captain Dyllbert has sent me a message?

No sir! **Not Captain Dyllbert!** This message is from...

... DYLLBERT THE PIRATE!!!

Dyllbert the Pirate!!! Odds-flippin'-bods!!!

Inevitably, Fairface eventually meets (and falls deeply in love with) the man she has sworn to destroy, Dyllbert the Pirate!

Will they fight to the death or will they marry and join forces? There is only one way to find out! Look out for the future 'Dyllbert the Pirate' Cartoon Book that tells their story.

Cookie Le Crumble

Cookie Le Crumble is a gigantic and fearsome looking French born cook who loves food and lives for his cooking.

Prior to becoming a cook however, Le Crumble was an aggressive French soldier. A major asset to the army in fact for, French enemies would invariably take just one look at Cookie's 'T. Rex' size... and surrender! (Who wouldn't!)

He was, nonetheless, involved in battles and, it was during a battle that Cookie lost his left hand.

Invalided out of the army, he eventually became a ship's cook after cleverly adapting a metal pudding basin to fit on his stump to accommodate a variety of cooking aids including a whisk!

Despite his outwardly enormous and frightening appearance, inwardly Cookie is really a pretty gentle, 'wouldn't hurt a fly' sort of guy. (Except when roused, then everybody ducks for cover!)

Don't miss Dyllbert's encounter with Cookie in Book Two.

The Legend of Dyllbert the Pirate

"First Sea Lord Henry Lord Melville is shocked by Dyllbert's turn to piracy and now looks for someone to blame ..."

Well, m'Lord Pudd! What are you going to do about it!

Er, about what, m'Lord Melville?

About Dyllbert stealing the Iron Pudding of course, you stupid Admiral!

How dare you sir! I am not a stupid Admiral!

No! Then who *was* the stupid Admiral who chose Dyllbert for the trials in the first place!

Er, (gulp) good point!

He must be hunted down gentlemen! I shall take the **VICTORY** ...

... and **scour the oceans of the world until I find him!** And when I do I will return to Portsmouth with the mutinous crew of The Iron Pudding, along with the head ...

... of that accursed, Flagship stealing, traitorous dog... **DYLLBERT THE PIRATE!!!**

Oddsbods!

END OF EPISODE ONE

Dyllbert the Pirate's Fact File

Not A patch on Nelson!

In June 1794, a joint British army/navy force attacked the French held island of Corsica.

A month later at Calvi on Corsica's north-western coast, Nelson himself was ashore directing the fire of a battery of cannon's landed from his command ship, 'Agamemnon', when a French Cannonball exploded nearby and threw sharp pieces of stone and gravel up into his face, permanently damaging his right eye. In typical Nelson fashion, he shrugged off the injury, continued with his duties and Calvi fell to the British.

Although sometimes portrayed in films and plays as wearing an eyepatch, there is no real evidence that he actually ever wore one. It is known however that he did make use of a green eyeshade that was sewn into the lining of his cocked hat!

Years later, during a sea battle in the Baltic with the Danes, Nelson used his blind eye to good advantage. Things had begun to go disasterously wrong for the British and Admiral Sir Hyde Parker (Nelson's superior), signalled to Nelson's flagship: 'Elephant' ordering him to break off the action and withdraw.

When informed of the signal, Nelson merely raised his telescope to his blind eye and said; "I really do not see the signal". Consequently the action continued and (luckily for the disobedient Nelson) the British finally won the day.

ATTENTION CREW!!
Keep a weather eye out for Book Two of
"The Legend of Dyllbert the Pirate"
entitled:
"The Capture of Cookie Le Crumble"